Sustaining Leadership

Sustaining Leadership

Renewing Your Strength and Sparkle

Peter Shaw

CANTERBURY
PRESS
Norwich

© Peter Shaw 2014

First published in 2014 by the Canterbury Press Norwich
Editorial Office
3rd Floor, Invicta House,
108–114 Golden Lane,
London EC1Y 0TG.

Canterbury Press is an imprint of Hymns Ancient & Modern Ltd
(a registered charity)
13A Hellesdon Park Road, Norwich,
Norfolk NR6 5DR, UK

www.canterburypress.co.uk

978 1 84825 596 8

British Library Cataloguing in Publication data

A catalogue record for this book is available
from the British Library

Typeset by Manila Typesetting Company
Printed and bound in Great Britain by
CPI Group (UK) Ltd, Croydon

Contents

To our grandchildren, that they may be sustained by those who love them and may sustain others in love and hope throughout their lives.

Acknowledgements

It has been a delight to write this book. As I look back over forty-two years of working life I am conscious that I have been sustained as a leader at key points by people who trusted in me and enabled me to focus on what is most important. Their sustaining of me came through asking good questions and enabling me to put different possibilities into context and see what might be future opportunities. They enabled me to handle the closing of doors and the slight opening of other possibilities.

I had the opportunity to move careers after thirty-two years in government and have now spent over ten years coaching individuals and teams and writing books. I observe others who have sustained their own values and leadership through switching between sectors or moving from paid to voluntary leadership roles.

A passion for me is to enable individuals to sustain and grow their love of life and to be an influence for good in their work, in their community and with their family and friends. I seek to work with those who want to sustain leadership in a constructive way, whatever their personal circumstances and whatever the pressures upon them. I have been inspired by many of the people I have had the privilege to work with.

In writing this book those who have had a particular influence upon my thinking have been Ruth Sinclair, Hilary Douglas, Zoë Stear, David Quine, John Goldring, Michael Tripp, Jeremy Oates and David Cracknell. They are all people who have sustained their leadership and their wider contribution through changing contexts and personal circumstances. Ruth, Hilary and Zoë have provided very helpful comments on the text of the book.

I am grateful to Una O'Brien who has written the Foreword to the book. Una is an inspiration to many as she leads a major government department through times of major change. She sustains others through her inspirational approach. No problem is insoluble to Una. She inspires others to bring the same determined and pragmatic approach.

I am very grateful to Jackie Tookey, who has not only typed the book with great care but has offered many very helpful comments about what I had written. Sonia John-Lewis has organized my life skilfully to give me time to write. Christine Smith has been a superb editor at Canterbury Press in giving me the freedom to write a series of books on aspects of leadership, with *Sustaining Leadership* following the *Reflective Leader* (written jointly with Alan Smith) and *The Emerging Leader* (written jointly with Colin Shaw). The fourth book in the sequence, *Wake up and Dream*, is the next project.

I am indebted to my family for giving me the space to write. Frances always brings practical wisdom as she and I talk about how we keep sustained in our sixties.

The book was written during a month when our second grandson was born. It was a delight when Daniel arrived, which certainly sustains us in looking positively to the future. The book is dedicated to our grandchildren, of whom the first two, Barney and Daniel, are already sources of great pleasure to us both.

Foreword

The demands of your work can feel tough and difficult. Life can feel unrelenting. You can be at risk of feeling you are not quite good enough.

We have all had moments when we feel 'in the grip'. Whatever sector we are in we can feel at the mercy of events with no time to reflect.

Peter's book speaks to leaders in all kinds of organisations. The book is full of practical wisdom and gentle coaching. Peter's book is affirming of what you have been seeking to do as a leader. It encourages you to be kind and self-compassionate to yourself and not condemnatory. The book is full of good, practical help to enable you to think constructively about your next steps.

Peter uses a practical framework of the four 'Rs' of reflect, reframe, rebalance and renew. I keep returning to Part 9 of the book which sets out how this framework of the four 'Rs' can be used effectively.

I see the fifth 'R' as resilience which links together, reflect, reframe, rebalance and renew. This book gives the reader the tools to be resilient. It encourages ingenuity in putting together a plan. It stresses the importance of both understanding yourself well, and reaching out to others so you can both sustain yourself and sustain those people who are important to you.

I have known Peter for ten years and feel sustained through regular conversation with Peter. View the book as a conversation with Peter which will sustain you through good moments and demanding times.

Reading this book will enable you to reflect, reframe, rebalance and renew in a way that will take your resilience to a higher level and enable you to see the future in both a realistic and a positive light.

Una O'Brien
Permanent Secretary
Department of Health
London, England

Introduction

You are part way through your working life. You want to continue to make a difference to the lives of individuals. There may be a lot of runway left in your current job or preferred activity. You might have to change direction because of new realities, but you still want to lead and influence others. You might feel stuck and discouraged.

You want to be sustained and energized. Your desire is to keep doing what you are good at and be stimulated by fresh ideas and new opportunities. Perhaps you can see a possible way ahead, or you may feel boxed in with limited prospects of moving into new spheres.

Expectations are rising. Technology means you have to work more quickly. There are more pressures, not fewer. Resources are tight. There is more to be done and less time to do it, but there is also an openness to change in you and others. Colleagues and clients are sometimes open to new ideas and you want to make the most of opportunities that are there.

You may love the work you do. It is fulfilling and is using your capabilities well. The question is: How do you decide between opportunities and sustain your energy?

Sometimes you feel encouraged by the difference you are able to make. On other occasions your head wants to drop. Your enthusiasm is not as great as it used to be. Life feels like hard work. How do you lift your spirits and feel sustained when it feels a struggle? What might inspire you and capture your imagination going forward? How do you get the spark back?

Perhaps it feels like a long haul. Keeping going as a leader is hard work, with not much light at the end of the tunnel. You enjoy the work – well, sort of. You get good feedback on the work you do, but the pace seems relentless and you need to keep moving. You see how you can make a difference, but it feels like an uphill struggle sometimes. You have a strong need for appreciation, which is not often forthcoming.

You want to feel endorsed and appreciated. You want to know you are not alone and that others have travelled the same route. You want to be encouraged and feel there are practical ideas you can latch on to to enable you to make the difference you want to make.

Perhaps in certain areas of your life you feel you are making good progress and are able to contribute well. In other areas you feel stuck and constrained. How best do you use the energy drawn from one area of life to sustain you in others? How best do you balance receiving encouragement and development in some spheres and having to give out more in others, with limited appreciation from those around you?

You are conscious that your energy and effectiveness are at their highest when you are feeling positive about the way forward in key areas of your life. There are always choices to be made about how you nurture energy in some areas and deploy it in others.

There is always going to be personal sadness to be handled alongside work and family life. Keeping your equilibrium through emotional ups and downs is a key element in sustaining leadership through demanding times.

The heart of this book is the value of creating a virtuous circle in which you *Reflect*, *Reframe*, *Rebalance* and *Renew*. The book takes the reader on a journey through this cycle. Under *Reflect* it looks at 'Where are you?' and 'Know what matters to you'. Within *Reframe* it considers, 'Keep open to what might be possible' and 'Know how you handle potential derailers'.

In *Rebalance* it looks at 'Stay professional and focused' and 'Embrace simplicity'. Under *Renew* it addresses 'Bring a lightness of touch' and 'Build for the future'. The last part, called 'Keep sustained', invites you to link together how you reflect, reframe, rebalance and renew.

The ideas in the book are relevant for leaders at any level part way through your career. You might be a senior leader or middle manager in a public, private or voluntary organization who is in a rewarding job but know that decisions need to be taken about how best to use time and energy. You might be conscious that the opportunity for promotion is limited and you have to sustain your leadership with limited prospects of promotion or a move into other senior roles.

You might be a senior member of a school's teaching staff, with limited scope to move to another role and needing to make choices about how you balance work, family and community activities. You might be the leader of a project and need to make choices about whether you stay in the same project area or seek to enter a related but different one.

You might be the vicar or minister of a church where you have been in the role for some time and expect to continue in it for the foreseeable future: you want to keep yourself and the organization fresh through bringing in new ideas. You might be a leader or manager in a charity where there is a long-term commitment to the work but only limited signs of progress: you need to decide whether to stay on or to seek to move to another charity.

You might be a specialist in a business area that is in gradual decline and where the long-term prospects are not good. You need to decide how to describe and develop your skills so that you can use them in a wider range of paid and unpaid activities.

This book seeks to be relevant to both individuals and groups. It could form the basis for coaching conversations or for discussion groups.

My hope is that the book will enable you to step into your future in a positive way, bringing a new curiosity about what might engage you, a new excitement about what might be possible and new hope about the difference you might be able to make in areas that are important to you.

I want to encourage you to be positive in the way you think about the future. There are going to be opportunities that might not be immediately obvious. There are going to be choices to be made about your priorities and your attitude. Do be open to ideas that catch your imagination and the pathways that might be ahead, then walk with expectation into your future.

Peter Shaw
Godalming, England
peteralanshaw@gmail.com

REFLECT

PART 1

WHERE ARE YOU?

When you look back you see the journey you have travelled. There have been highs and lows. You have climbed mountains and experienced tougher periods.

Perhaps now is a good moment to reflect on the journey so far and what might be to come. It is the time to take satisfaction in your contribution so far and to give thanks for the gifts you have been endowed with. It is also a moment to face up to and accept reality and do a stocktake about how your gifts and interests might translate into future possibilities.

1

Recognize your contribution so far

You might have reached a major milestone recently in your life. Perhaps you have recently had a significant birthday that ends with a five or a nought. You may have been in your current type of work for ten or twenty years and have begun to reflect on what it is all for.

There may be a risk of a dip in your motivation and enthusiasm. You might be beginning to think you are about to enter a midlife crisis, but dismiss that as too grandiose a description of what you are currently feeling. But there is a restlessness in you. Doubts appear about whether you have made the right choices about your career or your work. You are hesitant about your future in a way you had not been a decade earlier. You are in a reflective space with a risk of sinking into gloom and melancholy.

Where do you start in thinking about where you are and what next? A good starting point is to reflect on your journey so far and to remember the contribution you have made in different spheres. Recalling the contribution made in both work and personal lives reminds us where we have made a difference and where our contribution has been appreciated.

Taking stock can remind us that we have made a contribution to our family. We have provided encouragement to our siblings or support to the children in our lives. We have given pleasure to our parents and to those in the community where we grew up who follow our lives with interest. We have enjoyed friendships where there has been mutual encouragement and a sense of adventure and laughter.

We have perhaps contributed to a sports team or a community group where there has been success and laughter. We may have contributed to our local church whether as a member of the core team or as an occasional participant willing to help in practical ways.

In our work we have made a contribution that has been appreciated by others. Some of it may seem long gone and forgotten. But there are letters we keep, or performance reviews we retain, or e-mails that we have not deleted that remind us of the esteem in which we were held and the contribution we made.

As a teacher you can take pride in those who learnt from what you taught them. As a manager you can recall those who grew in confidence because of the mentoring you gave them. As an advisor you can remember those who made better decisions having talked through their options with you.

Sometimes our contribution is obvious and memorable. I wrote the report that changed the direction that the company took. I did the operation that saved someone's life. I prepared someone for a major interview and they got the job. I designed a piece of software that has benefited many people. Sometimes our contribution will have been less obvious. A word of encouragement or the practical assistance has been long forgotten, but you can take satisfaction in the way gentle suggestions or words of encouragement have lifted someone's confidence and enabled them to move forward in a more cheerful and purposeful way.

We can remember contributions where we have responded to someone's emotional needs or spiritual journey. We have helped them see life and its mysteries in a new way. Being alongside someone at times of need or when they are searching can have a profound effect upon them and on us.

Oliver had been the accountant in a small firm for a number of years. After having studied for a geography degree he enjoyed his accountancy training and quickly took on positions of responsibility. But he had been in the same role at his current company for six years and had begun to wonder what the future might hold. He knew he had to think more constructively about the future.

When Oliver reflected on his journey he was reminded why he had become an accountant and how he enjoyed much of the work. He had made an important contribution in different jobs in ensuring there was a good financial discipline and proper budget planning. He had ensured that the firm was financially sound and that resources were used well.

Oliver took pride in his young family and loved playing football with the boys. He felt he was making a good contribution as a dad while recognizing that balancing work and home was not always straightforward. Reminding himself of the contribution that he had made in different spheres enabled him to think constructively about what the future might hold.

Some points for reflection

- What contributions at work have given you the most pleasure?
- What contributions in the wider community are you most pleased about?
- What contribution within your family gives you most satisfaction?
- When have you been at your best in balancing these different contributions?

2

Give thanks for your gifts

We may see our contribution as ordinary and not special. We may see others gliding past us on stellar careers. We brought lots of energy in the past but seem to be finding it difficult to raise a similar level of enthusiasm going forward.

But what are the gifts in us that have brought us this far? We cannot be devoid of strengths. There must be competences in us or we would not have been able to take the steps we have completed on our journey.

There may be gifts in us we have taken for granted or fail to see. On a good day we recognize our intellectual qualities, including our ability to assess figures, facts and situations. On other occasions we recognize our emotional awareness about people, relationships and dynamics.

Sometimes we have a breakthrough and recognize we are good at something and hold firmly on to recognizing that quality. We are good at cheering people up, giving practical guidance, enabling someone to prioritize or helping people to use their time and energy better.

Sometimes the gifts we bring are technical and hard-edged. We know how to manage projects, plan a budget, solve IT problems or run a meeting. Sometimes our gifts are softer skills in terms of motivating individuals to learn, enabling a team to work together effectively, or motivating a group of individuals to see possibilities they had dismissed before.

Sometimes we bring a gift enabling someone to become more spiritually aware of what is most important to them and where they can make their biggest contribution. The gift of spiritual awareness is about being present with someone in such a way that there is a holistic bringing together of their understanding of their place in the world, and what matters to them most in their personal, community, work and family contexts.

Often we do not appreciate our gifts and qualities. We take for granted the fact that we can plan a sequence of practical steps, contribute well to a meeting, draft a summary of conclusions or influence someone to change their mind. Even when others tell us we are good at something we can often dismiss their feedback and not recognize the qualities in us. It can be very enlightening to ask someone what they particularly appreciate about your approach and contribution, provided you are ready to believe what we hear.

When I work with groups and teams I often encourage people to give each other positive affirmation. I will ask people in pairs to say to the other person what they most appreciate about their qualities and their approach, and then to listen as they receive their own feedback from their colleague. I then invite them to talk to other people, one by one, in the group and believe the pattern of affirming comments they are receiving.

Oliver was getting bored with being an accountant. He seemed to be always giving the same messages about financial discipline. The pattern in the way resources were spent during a year did not seem to vary very much other than handling the periodic nasty surprise. Oliver was in danger of getting grumpy.

Oliver was slightly taken aback when a colleague thanked him for the way he had built a consensus in a meeting. Oliver had seen himself as an accountant rather than a consensus builder. As Oliver reflected on other situations he could see how he had built a sense of shared endeavour in a range of different situations. Perhaps he did have a gift of enabling people to work together to find an agreed way forward.

Perhaps that was a gift he could build on going forward. Oliver was curious about what others thought about his contribution. He asked three or four trusted colleagues to give him feedback on where his contribution made the biggest difference. He was taken by surprise that the comments were not about his technical expertise but about the way he had influenced and motivated his colleagues to find new ways of solving problems. Oliver was pleasantly surprised by the feedback that his gifts were wider than he had perhaps assumed.

Some points for reflection

- What are the technical competences you are most proud of?
- What are the gifts of emotional awareness you might not always fully appreciate?
- What are the gifts of insight or spiritual awareness you perhaps don't fully acknowledge?
- How would other people describe the gifts you possess?

3

Accept your reality

Whatever our current situation there will be an emotional overlay. The facts of our current reality may be that we have a part-time job, a partner and two children and have lived in the same house for five years. Our emotional reality might be a fulfilment and joyfulness in our work and a delight in our family. On the other hand, our emotional reality might be frustration in our work, ambivalence about our key relationships and resentment about certain members of our family.

Our spiritual reality might be a strong sense of vocation and clarity of purpose in our lives. Or the spiritual reality might be an inner battle between constructive and destructive forces that are eating up our sense of hope and purpose. Our financial reality might be the satisfaction of living within our financial means, or it might be a frustrated desire to have a better standard of living.

Before we can move on we need to take stock of what is our current reality. In our workplace, are the needs for our skills rising or falling? Are people prepared to buy the services we offer? Do we need to retrain or readjust the focus of our work so that we are marketable?

If you are a mining engineer and all the local mines are closing, the harsh reality is that you need either to use your engineering skills in other industries or move to an area where the skill of a mining engineer continues to be in demand. However much current reality hurts it is a given. There is little point in wasting emotional energy railing against external factors that have 'taken away my job'.

When you feel cross that your previous reality is coming to an end, allow yourself to go into an empty space and rail against the injustice for, say, half an hour and when that time has elapsed tell yourself it is time to move on. This may be a process you need to repeat on more than one occasion.

Often it is helpful to ask a friend, 'What do you observe as the new reality I need to face up to?' The direct comments from a trusted other can help you face up to the harsh reality you might want to ignore but can't.

Facing up to harsh reality might be about recognizing the failing health of a parent, the decline in a particular community group you are part of or the shrinking in numbers of an ageing church membership. Harsh reality might be accepting your own human frailty and periodic forgetfulness.

The paradox is that as we accept harsh reality we are more likely to be open-minded to see opportunities. When we are frustrated about our current reality our sense of curiosity and wonder is squeezed out. As we come to terms with our current reality our freshness of thinking and curiosity can burst out and we can begin to see new avenues and new ways of thinking ahead.

Oliver recognized that he had to come to terms with the fact that he was increasingly bored doing basic, financial analysis. But good financial discipline in the organization where he was the accountant was crucial. The harsh reality was that he had to continue to do the boring bits of the job, but he also began to explore how he could become more involved in planning ahead. He sought to contribute to strategic conversations more purposefully. He began to make a contribution that seemed to be appreciated in looking for future opportunities for the business to become both more efficient and more effective.

Once Oliver accepted the reality of the need to do the day job well he ceased to be frustrated with the routine. It was as if a black cloud had been lifted and he was more excited about the wider influence he could have within the business in helping it grow. He shifted from describing himself as 'the boring accountant' to 'the agitator accountant' because of the way he was prompting people to think about using resources in a new, more stimulating way.

Some points for reflection

- See accepting your reality as releasing you for the future.
- What current realities are frustrating you? Can you diffuse that frustration?
- Can you see examples of where you have accepted more readily your new reality over recent months and moved on?
- What is the new reality you are finding difficult to accept but need to accept?
- What is the liberation that might result from trying to seek opportunities and not just painful realities?

4

Do a stocktake

An accurate stocktake covers highs and lows. It includes the best of moments and the worst of moments. It incorporates the mountain tops and the devastating lows.

A good stocktake is honest about reality but not blinkered or prejudiced in its approach. The good things are seen for what they are. The bad things are viewed honestly. But the lens that is used is clear.

An honest stocktake puts to one side the distortion that frustration or bitterness can bring. A good stocktake is neither through 'rose tinted glasses' nor through an insistence of morbid darkness.

A good stocktaker involves the asking of honest, thorough questions such as:

- What was really going on in my life?
- What was inspiring me and bringing out the best in me?
- What gave me energy, hope and conviction for the future?
- Who helped to lift my spirits and enabled me to be the best I could be?

Part of a good stocktake is to look at the darker side, asking ourselves, honestly, questions like:

- Where and why did I stand back from opportunities?
- What were the demons in me I was unable to tame?

- When, through my attitudes, did I create a self-fulfilling prophecy of doom?
- When was I my own worst enemy?

As we reflect on our journey so far we are looking at both facts and emotions. There will always be events we can celebrate when we have been at our best and made a difference. These will be times when we have been a source of encouragement and renewal for others, or moments when we have received affirmation or recognition from others and we feel proud that we have made a valuable contribution.

But we might also be conscious of when we have stood back when we could have intervened. There may have been times when we were indulgent and enjoyed false pride too much, or times when we have not fully taken on board our responsibilities.

Taking stock is about recognizing when we have been at our best and celebrating our success and the impact we have had. Taking stock is also about facing up to our own shortcomings and failings. It is not about wallowing in our own frailty, but it is recognizing the reality of these highs and lows.

A good stocktake leads to seeing how life's journey has developed understanding and insights within us. Harsh reality has sharpened the steel in us and built our resilience. Harsh reality might also have left wounds that we know we have to protect and be mindful of. Often the injured part of the body has recovered so it is stronger than parts of the body that have not been subjected to intense aggravation.

A good stocktake involves standing outside yourself and possibly listing the defining moments in your life that have strengthened and shaped you. It can be well worth listing ten defining moments, five that were highs and a second five that were lows.

Talking with a friend, mentor, coach or colleague asking them to help enable you to explore these defining moments can help put them into a new and more creative light. Looking back provides a mirror on your life and allows the linking together of highs and lows to show the pattern that has been emerging. One technique is metaphorically to look back ten years and see the trends in your life. And then look forward over the next ten years to see where the developing trends and pattern may now be taking you.

Introspection when doing a stocktake is fine and helpful up to a point. But there is a moment when it is timely to say, 'Enough is enough; it is now time to move forward', informed by the reflection and energized by the belief that life experience often prepares us for the futures we seek to move into or that open up before us.

> *When Oliver went for long walks with his friend Mike he began to talk about his life as an accountant. It had given him moments of satisfaction. He felt his contribution had benefited the small firm where he worked. He saw how he had become more strategic and influential over the years. Through Mike's gentle questioning Oliver reflected on his emotional journey, as well as his progression through the firm. He had enjoyed the external relations and mentoring of staff much more in the last two or three years. He understood more fully some of his frustrations about the technical side of the job. He could describe himself as a more grounded and influential leader than he had been in his early days when he could be a rather blunt finance specialist.*
>
> *The conversation with Mike helped Oliver hold together the good and the bad times in his job and how it had shaped him. He was not sure what the future would hold but he felt in a better equilibrium as he began to think through future possibilities.*

Some points for reflection

When you do a stocktake:

- Explore your emotions but do not be dominated by them.
- Be as objective as possible in looking at the highs and the lows.
- Use a friend, mentor, coach or good colleague to help you explore how you have been shaped by your experience.
- Allow yourself to believe that progress comes through tough times just as much as through success.

PART 2

KNOW WHAT MATTERS TO YOU

When we are daunted about what the future might hold and how we are going to be sustained, it is worth standing still to reflect on what matters to you. This reflection is not about what others might think matters to you or what mattered to you ten years ago. An honest reflection of what really matters to you now is an essential process when thinking about sustaining your leadership.

As part of that consideration we explore in this part: What mountains do you want to climb? What do you want to leave behind? Where does work fit into the rest of life? and What do you want your legacy to be?

5

What mountains do you want to climb?

When we were younger we might have decided to climb mountains just because they were there. We would choose the most direct route to the top whether or not it had the best footholds. In our youth, climbing a mountain did not exhaust us physically or emotionally, or so we want to believe in retrospect.

We might sometimes have climbed hills without a great deal of preparation, relying on our physical fitness and good companions to get us to the top. Hard experience taught us that a waterproof anorak and good-quality boots were essential. In the days when we felt macho we did not bother with waterproof trousers. But a few heavy colds later, and after a bout of pneumonia, I always have a pair of waterproof trousers in the rucksack. Walking up previous mountains has taught us to expect that when we reach the brow of a hill another brow will come into sight. We have taught ourselves to pace our energies and not to assume that we will reach our destination in record-breaking time.

We have learnt that climbing a mountain involves good preparation, bringing the right equipment, planning the route, bringing the right supplies, having good companions and knowing the distances that we can readily handle. We have taught ourselves to cope with torrential rain, limited visibility, piercing wind or biting cold. We have got used to pacing our energies, keeping going when exhausted, focusing on the destination and allowing ourselves small treats to encourage us. For me an essential part of a long walk is a supply of 'fudge bars'.

They are a strong memory from childhood and are always a boost emotionally as well as physically.

But what are the next mountains we want to climb? Perhaps they are physical hills. We want to prove to ourselves that we can still get to the top of an alpine peak or a Scottish Munro or one of the Lake District hilltops. We went up Great Gable on our honeymoon: perhaps we should go up there again forty years later. When our children were aged seven, nine and eleven we walked up Ben Nevis, Scafell Pike and Snowdon, encouraging them on their way to the top. If we did these walks again these three children, now twenty-plus years later, would be at the top first with Frances and I way behind.

Do we now attempt the same mountains we went up before or do we seek different mountains? We want to see what the view is like from different vantage points. You have been a good parent of a four year old: being the parent of a sixteen year old is challenging in a very different way. We have been a successful project leader but know that the mountain we need to climb is leading project leaders well rather than leading a project ourselves. The mountain for us might be learning to steer others and not just relying on our own capabilities.

The mountain we want to climb might be one that enables us to bring a more strategic perspective and see the whole vista. We know we must not get so bogged down in the detail. We need to be able to make judgements relying on less direct first-hand experience than before. We have to follow our intuition while testing out and then making decisions on the basis of less certainty than before.

The mountains we want to climb might be in the workplace or a context we currently occupy as we aspire for promotion. Or we might want to climb a completely different mountain in a different location and area of work. We might want to switch career or put an increasing amount of our energies into our voluntary responsibilities. Or family responsibilities may mean that there is a new, demanding personal life where we have to apply our energy, patience and time. Perhaps we have ageing parents with dementia where the mountain we have to climb is one of patience and forbearance.

Alison had been a primary-school teacher for twenty years. She had enjoyed working with generations of children and had become a deputy head. The choice for Alison was whether she aspired to become a head teacher of a primary school or whether she took on a greater leadership role in her church. Various people at the church had spoken to her about the possibility of doing the training to become a non-stipendiary minister. She recognized that it was unrealistic to do both.

Alison's first question was whether either of these was the thing to do. She had two children with whom she had a good relationship. Alison knew that as they went through their teenage years there would be demands on her time and emotions that would be unpredictable, but knew she wanted to climb another mountain and had the support of those around her to so do. She began to explore both the possibility of being a primary-school head teacher and the possibility of training to become a non-stipendiary minister. A couple of good friends helped her work through the options.

Some points for reflection

- What had enabled me to climb mountains before? Are those capabilities still there?
- Am I looking to climb a similar or very different mountain going forward?
- How might I decide which type of mountain to climb?
- Who are the people I can talk possibilities through with most helpfully?

6

What do you want to leave behind?

As I write this chapter the media is full of articles about Nelson Mandela. In the 1980s there was a sense of hopelessness that surrounded South African politics in what most accepted as the last days of the Apartheid era. Few could see any way forward other than serious and bloody violence as the white supremacists were forced to relinquish power. But Nelson Mandela rewrote the country's future when he resisted the two extremes of acquiescence and retribution.

Nelson Mandela left behind violence and retribution as the ways forward. He also left behind the acquiescence of previous generations. His focus on both truth and reconciliation had profound implications for the creation of a new democracy that hardly anyone thought would be possible. Nelson Mandela brought a unique combination of a firm belief in reconciliation combined with the leaving behind of past attitudes. Mandela's approach was informed partly by his Christian understanding of the centrality of both courage and forgiveness. His was a remarkable story of the leaving behind of any sense of anger after twenty-seven years in prison.

The twenty-seven years in prison had enabled Nelson Mandela to reflect on and decide what he wanted to leave behind and what was strengthening him going forward. There are times when we can feel boxed in as if we were in a cell on Robben Island. Perhaps rather than feeling frustrated about being locked in a cell it were better to use that time of isolation to reflect on what we want to leave behind.

What is the sense of injustice or anger or frustration that is holding us back and eating up our energy? So often it is the emotions that burn within us that are ultimately destructive and that we need to come to terms with and then leave behind. Sometimes the sense of anger needs to be examined, dissected, put in a box and vehemently thrown over the edge of a cliff.

Sometimes by virtue of our background we can feel inhibited in some situations. I was brought up in a small town in Yorkshire. My father died when I was seven and financial resources at home were limited. There was sometimes a danger of feeling as if I was 'hard done by from Yorkshire'. Two bosses early in my working life told me firmly to leave that attitude behind and recognize that I had a good career ahead of me.

In the early days of a career the aspiration to reach the top might be an important driver. But as others get promoted faster than us the notion that we could become the chief executive gradually disappears. We have to leave behind the ambition of reaching the top of the organization or else we will gradually become jaundiced and disappointed. But that does not mean leaving behind any sense of ambition. It is about recalibrating ambition so it continues to be stretching but is rooted in realism.

Sometimes we need to be open to leave behind our attitudes in relation to others as we see them change and become increasingly effective or influential. Perhaps we have partly written someone off and need to leave behind a half-formed impression: we can delight in being surprised by someone's progress when they have learnt from experience.

Sometimes we have to leave behind an overly positive view about an individual or a situation. Our belief that an individual could solve their own problems may have to be revised if there has been a sequence of failed attempts to do so.

Perhaps what we most often need to leave behind are attitudes in ourselves that become outdated. We need to be open for our minds and hearts to be changed as we see the good and wholesome in people drawn out and applied in bringing hope and renewal to both individuals and communities.

> *Alison knew that she needed to leave behind a fixed notion that she would only be successful if she became a primary-school head teacher. She also knew that she needed to leave behind a previous assumption that the best church leaders were male. Friends kept telling her that she had gifts that were equally applicable to church leadership as to school leadership. Alison recognized that she needed to move on from previous assumptions or ambitions and look in a dispassionate way at whether the right next step was to prepare to become a primary-school head or to seek to train to be a non-stipendiary lay minister in her local church.*
>
> *It was when Alison left behind the driven ambition to be a primary-school head that she was able to look at these two options in a more measured way. She drew on advice from friends and imagined herself in these two very different roles. Alison then decided that she would seek to enter training to be a lay minister. She had a peace of mind about this venture because she had worked through some of the dominant emotions that had previously gripped her.*

Some points for reflection

- Reassess what attitudes you want to take with you and what you want to leave behind.
- What attitudes do you hold that are now outdated?
- What sense of ambition needs to be recalibrated?

- What self-beliefs grip you in a way that inhibits your thinking?
- What attitudes are best left behind if your thinking for the future is to be liberated?

7

Where does work fit into the rest of life?

We know what matters to us now when we look at how we spend our time and energy. We may feel we are a captive of circumstances, but we are making choices all the time about our use of time and energy. We are also making choices every day about our *attitude* to the way we spend that time and energy.

If you are spending fifty hours a week working, your attitude may be that you are hard done by and resent spending ten more hours at work than you are paid for. On the other hand your reaction might be that it is a privilege to be able to work in an interesting and stimulating environment.

Work might fit in well to the rest of life because those who are closest to us have made choices that enable us to give time and energy to work. Perhaps we take their goodwill for granted sometimes. Perhaps a change in our partner's circumstances means that a previous equilibrium has to be reassessed. Our partner's taking on a bigger role at work, or needing to spend more time with aged parents, can mean that a reassessment in our priorities is necessary.

Part of reassessing where work fits into the rest of life is looking at the financial equilibrium we want to establish. What are the financial parameters we want to set? Where ideally do we want to live and in what type of house? Do we want to be paying school fees or private health insurance? What are our aspirations for holidays, our future pension and what amount of capital would we want to pass on to our children? Or are these considerations not important to us? Are we content to take one step at a time without a detailed, long-term plan for the future?

It can be a good exercise to think about what you would choose to do if you had a free half-day. For some the answer will be doing some reading or activity relevant to work. For others the answer will be to spend time with family and friends. For others it will be time spent on a personal interest. The instinctive answer to this question can give important clues about your preferred priorities going forward.

For some people the right conclusion is for work to fill a bigger part in their lives than now. For a parent who has spent a number of years bringing up children, returning to paid employment can provide a new level of engagement with other people and a different way of being a good parent. For other people the appropriate next step is to reduce their commitment to work as 'the be all and end all' and use their time more efficiently and effectively in the work they do.

I have coached a number of senior women who have been excellent parents as well as committed and effective leaders. These women have developed a sophistication in the use of their time and energy that is impressive. They have developed the ability to work on a number of plans in tandem and switch in a focused way from one activity to another. They have often developed very adaptable means of fitting work into the rest of life.

Now might be the moment to be creative about deciding how work best fits into the rest of life. It might mean switching work priorities. It could mean being more flexible in your work hours. It will certainly mean being more focused and using time more effectively. It could mean using electronic means of communication in a more creative and flexible way.

It is often too easy to complain that I am too busy and cannot fit work into the rest of life. The most productive approach is to reflect on how best might I link together my different priorities. How best can I find an equilibrium that uses my time and energy well? In what ways am I going to use technology in a different way? How am I going to be flexible and adaptable? How am I going to work well in new ways with others who are also addressing the same issues?

Alison knew that she needed to talk with her daughters about when they most needed their mum around and when they would be content for her to be less available. The two girls were remarkably grown up in saying when it was essential for their mum to be there. They took pride in the fact that their mum was the deputy head of a school. This gave them a certain street cred. When their mum talked about doing some training at college, the daughters took pride in the fact that their mum was going to be a student too.

Alison thought through how best she could fit the training to be a lay minister into the weekly schedule. She invested in a new laptop and was also willing to invest in the textbooks. Alison recognized that she would need to be less perfectionist in the way her house looked. Her daughters saw this as a potential benefit and hoped that their mum's taking on of more responsibilities would mean that she did not hassle her daughters quite so much to keep their bedrooms tidy.

Some points for reflection

- How might you adapt the time you spend at work so it is more productive?

- How might you use information technology more effectively to enable you to use your time better?
- With whom do you need to renegotiate the use of time and energy in a way that benefits you and them?
- What are the fixed points about the use of time and energy that you need to stick to more rigidly?

8

What difference do you want to make?

In my first career as a civil servant in the UK government, when I was at the Department for Education, the difference I wanted to make was about contributing to the enhancement of educational opportunity and attainment for pupils and students of all ages. In the last eleven years as an executive coach the difference I have wanted to make has been stimulating individuals and teams to step up to take on bigger responsibilities effectively.

The difference I want to make now is enhancing someone's belief that they can have an impact. My role is to enable individuals and teams to link together their vision about what is possible in the future, the values that drive them, what type of value-added they are going to bring and what are the sources of their vitality that they want to grow and nurture.

Many people go through the transition from an initial phase of work where they make a difference by virtue of what they individually do. In the second phase more of their impact comes through enabling others to have the impact they want to have. The research scientist in the first phase of their career is having an impact because of the personal research they do. It is their mental creativity and their purposeful endeavour that lead to the scientific breakthrough. Their productivity is very individual and personable. Later in their career the research scientist has a bigger impact through the team they lead and through inspiring and enabling the next generation of research scientists to push the boundaries of understanding.

When you reflect on how you sustain your leadership responsibilities it is worth reflecting on what is changing about the difference you want to make. It could be that the priority of your work is moving from the short term to the longer team. It might be that you want to influence the strategic direction of the organization you are part of, or you might want to focus hard on one particular outcome that you are determined to see happen.

You might feel swept along by economic or political change that you have no control over. You work in a school where another phase of political priorities is sweeping through like a remorseless wave. You might be working in a hospital where financial pressures are driving a different way of doing things. You may be working on a major capital project where a demanding client has set rigid and unrelenting expectations. But in each situation it is worth asking the question: What is the scope for me to make a difference? What opportunities are opened up by the latest, political fashion or economic imperative? How can I make myself useful so that I can make a difference and take pride in the impact that I can have?

I am surprised when I meet people ten-plus years on from our having worked together in government when they remark upon the mentoring influence I had on them. I did not realize at the time that I was enabling them to have confidence in their own abilities and to develop their own approach and impact.

It may not always be obvious what difference we are making. If we are looking for instant results we are going to be disappointed. The most satisfying impact we can have on others is long term in respect of their confidence and competences, the results only showing after a number of years.

Perhaps we can delight more often in the long-term impact we can have. If we set off in the next phase of our life thinking that we are going to invest in the next generation and encourage them on their own leadership journeys, we will be making

33

an investment without knowing its consequences. Making a difference might be about nurturing the long-term aspirations of the younger people in our lives, be they in our families, our community or the workplace.

Alison weighed up what long-term difference she wanted to make. As a deputy head in a primary school she had a big influence on the way things were done in the school and how people worked together. Being the head would give her ultimate responsibility and allow her to set priorities, but she already had considerable influence in ways that were very significant in the staff room. As a lay minister, Alison would also have the opportunity to make a difference in the local church with people of a variety of age groups.

Alison saw for her the benefit of being able to make a difference in two different spheres with two different age groups. She thought this balance of working in two different communities would enable her to keep her equilibrium more easily in balance. She felt relaxed that she had made the right decision in taking forward the training to become a lay minister alongside continuing as the deputy head of the primary school.

Some points for reflection

- In which two or three areas do you want to make a difference going forward?
- In what ways do those areas complement each other?
- How much do you want to make a difference through what you do and how much through what you enable others to do?

- Looking forward ten years, what would give you the greatest satisfaction in the way others describe your influence upon them?
- How is the difference you want to make shifting in a constructive way?

REFRAME

PART 3

KEEP OPEN TO WHAT MIGHT BE POSSIBLE

In mid-career we can feel constrained and boxed in. Responsibilities as a parent or to parents are long term. There are constraints about geography, time and energy. But what might be possible?

This part explores what might be possible going forward and what opportunities might be there. It starts with recognizing the bigger picture and then looking for different angles and being curious. It addresses prioritizing your own development and then being ready for opportunities.

9

Recognize the bigger picture

Life is changing rapidly around us. The revolution in digital technology is changing how we communicate with each other, how information is processed and how decisions are made. The global economy means that the impact of economic change in one part of the world impacts quickly on apparently unrelated geographies and economies.

Confidence in investment decisions oscillates at an unprecedented rate. Social change has happened at a profound level in the last sixty years, affecting attitudes to work, family, parenting, relationships, the role of women, as well as attitudes to race, disability and sexuality. You began your work in one world and you now find yourself in a very different world. At one level you feel excited and liberated by the changes. At another level it leaves you feeling uncertain about your own future.

Twenty years ago you might have expected a career for life with a decent pension at the end of it. Now those assumptions have long gone and we are living in a more fluid and uncertain world, but the bigger-picture changes do have their benefits. Gone are the assumptions that limit what women can aspire to. Flexible work patterns are much more conducive to family arrangements that allow both partners to work. Information technology has resulted in a much greater flexibility being possible in the way work is organized.

The availability of insight and experience from across the world means a much greater openness to new ways of doing things and a greater acceptance that traditional patterns of organizing activity and thinking need to change. Big organizations have learnt that they have to be adaptable and work with myriad partners.

The bigger-picture changes may seem daunting, uncertain and unwelcoming. Relentless stories about economic pressures sap our confidence in the future. Media bashing of one profession after another means we question whether there are meaningful values in public life or in different groups we used to respect. But just when we might allow despondency about human nature to sap any optimism about the future, we hear stories about enterprise that has worked, reconciliation that has renewed relationships or the persistent contribution of probation officers, social workers or prison chaplains that has helped kindle hope and new attitudes and patterns of behaviour.

Holding a bigger picture in your mind involves believing that there are aspects of the bigger-picture changes that will have a productive impact in the longer term. The opportunity to travel much more has opened up an understanding of different cultures. Through the internet we can understand much more about creative ideas in different parts of the world. Pictures of famine and destruction bring even more sharply into focus the effect of misuse of resources and the impact of evil intent.

Perhaps we have to allow the bigger picture to help stimulate us to think about what might be possible and how we might want to contribute going forward. This is not about dramatically changing the world but it is about applying the understanding that comes from a greater appreciation of changes and trends in the wider world to inspire our thinking and our actions.

With three children now aged around thirty, I am conscious of the responsibility on emerging leaders in a demanding and fast-changing world. Seeing the pressures they face has been an inspiration to me in seeking to mentor a new generation of leaders thirty to forty years younger than me. Perhaps an element in finding our place in the bigger picture is recognizing the contribution we can make to mentor the next generation. This mentoring might come through our role as parents but it can also be part of our contribution in the local community or in the workplace.

Perhaps mentoring others keeps us grounded as we see the bigger picture in which we can play a part. For example, a friend well on track to become a judge spends a good chunk of the weekend coaching a football team of eleven year olds. A civil servant with high potential works every weekend with Air Cadets. The chief of staff to the chief executive in a major national charity spends Sunday morning leading a group of eight and nine year olds in the local church. All these people are engaged in their work on the bigger picture but are grounded in their thinking about life through coaching and mentoring young people. For each of them the coaching work they do helps them bring a practical realism about life to their leadership responsibilities in their work.

> *Bob was an IT technician in an international company who got a lot of satisfaction out of his work. He was regularly called upon to solve problems both at work and in the local community. He had a reputation for fixing things quickly and efficiently, but there was a risk he would get bored with this reputation as a fixer. He could see the potential for information technology to be used much more effectively in his workplace, in the community and in families. He got agreement from his employer to visit some other organizations to see how they had used information technology to both increase effectiveness and reduce internal friction. Bob was fascinated to explore how you combine face-to-face interaction effectively with digital interaction to enable*

decisions to be made constructively and implemented in an effective and harmonious way.

He was also fascinated by how different organizations were trying to relate to customers in a human and open way while still using information technology well. He was horrified by the type of automated messages that were often used by companies who pretended to want the custom of their callers but were blatantly pushing them to communicate by the web rather than through voice communication. Bob was excited to explore both within his work and in his community how oral and electronic communication could complement each other better.

Some points for reflection

- How best do we recognize the bigger picture?
- What are the changes in the wider world that are most likely to affect you?
- What are the economic and technological changes that will have unavoidable impact on the way you live your life?
- What are the values that are most important to you that you want to be rooted in as you live through economic, political and technological change?
- What are the changes in the bigger landscape that excite you most?

10

Look for different angles
and be curious

Curiosity may have killed the cat but curiosity keeps us fresh
and alert about what might be the opportunities going forward.
As soon as we stop being curious about what is going on in the
wider world we can become ossified in our approach. If we are
curious about how other people lead and think we are always
going to be gleaning thoughts and ideas from those with a different perspective.

When I am working with someone who experiences another
person as rigid and fixed in their views, I invite the person I am
working with to stand in the shoes of this other person. I might
invite them to do some role play in which they describe to their
colleagues what the world is like from the perspective of this
apparently difficult interlocutor. As soon as someone begins
to stand in the shoes of another person and express views as if
they were them, it often becomes clearer why the person thinks
in the way they do.

When we meet the most blinkered of people, the more we
can be curious about why they think the way they do the better
we will understand their motivations and their likely behaviour
in different situations. If you feel stuck in a particular organization, can you try and visit other similar organizations to see
how similar or different they are? If you work in a hospital,
spending time in a different hospital can provide you with new
ideas to try out. Being immersed in a different hospital might

lead you to be more confident in what you do in your job and enable you to see fresh ways of tackling difficult issues.

If you are feeling a bit stale, spending a week or a month on assignment at a different organization, or at a different site within the same organization, can provide a freshness of understanding that is far more stimulating than attending a few 'talking head' lectures.

Sometimes being curious about your own capabilities can lead you to trying different approaches. Perhaps you might volunteer to go on a community engagement board, or speak about the job you do at a school or college or offer to do a presentation about a particular piece of work you have been engaged in. You might offer to talk to a community group about the work you do.

You may be nervous and surprised by the reaction. You may find that you know more than you think and can articulate more clearly than you had thought what you are trying to achieve in your work. Putting yourself into exposed situations can demonstrate to you that you have strengths you had not appreciated. Perhaps you are a much better public speaker than you had thought. Perhaps you are far better at answering questions than you ever anticipated. Maybe you are going to surprise yourself and be encouraged about what type of activities you could build into your job going forward.

Looking for different angles might involve envisaging yourself in very different roles. The frustrated engineer might want to think through what it would be like teaching technology at a secondary school. A financial manager might want to think about how they might want to use their disciplined thinking as a project manager. A nurse who enjoys talking with patients might want to think about doing a counselling course and move into full-time counselling.

Being curious can involve thinking through how you might apply the gifts you have in a different context. It is not about ignoring your competences, it is about thinking through to what extent they are transferable and how they might be applied in a different but related sphere.

A lake can look very different depending on the vantage point. Our capabilities may look very different to different people. Part of being curious is asking other people for their perceptions about our capabilities. Normally when we invite these comments there will be a pattern, but we will be surprised by the comments of some, which will give us an interesting and different perspective and stimulate us to think through how we might apply our strengths in new ways.

Bob had always seen himself as an IT technician. He enjoyed solving other people's problems. But he could often see why a problem had happened and had ideas about how systems could be configured in such a way that these problems would not arise. When he was working in a medium-sized firm on a contract, he talked to the IT manager about his ideas. Initially the IT manager looked uninterested, but gradually he came to appreciate Bob's wisdom. The IT manager invited Bob to work with him on the design of a new system. Bob was relishing the opportunity to move from focusing purely on problem solving to a greater focus on design.

Bob was curious about how other organizations dealt with similar issues. He followed up a number of contacts and built a much clearer understanding of what had worked or not worked in different sectors. A couple of years ago his curiosity was purely about matters of details. Now his curiosity was much wider as he took his structured thinking into designing structures and systems where practical problems were minimized.

Some points for reflection

- How ready are you to look for different angles?
- Reflect on what makes you curious and how you follow up that curiosity.
- Invite others to comment on the particular capabilities you bring.
- Deliberately look at issues you are dealing with from a high vantage point and from different angles.
- See curiosity as a virtue and not a distraction.

11

Prioritize your own development

Recently someone said to me that they were now fifty-two and too old to learn new ways. I said that I did not believe them, and began to talk through with them some possible ways they might continue to learn and grow in understanding. Someone else recently said to me that at sixty-five they were now completely set in their ways. I pointed out that they were travelling to different places, were using the internet much more and were in close touch with their grandchildren.

Sometimes it is convenient to regard ourselves as too old to learn new ways. It provides a ready-made excuse to resist learning. If we say we are too old to learn, whether we be forty, fifty or sixty, we are limiting our horizons unnecessarily.

The evidence for most of us is that we are continually learning. Most of us use information technology more effectively that we did a year ago. This personal development might come through necessity or through following the example of an enthusiastic younger member of the family. Most of us are learning and adapting more quickly than we realize. All of us have the capacity to do so.

Perhaps we might not feel we are learning a lot in our current work situation. But in our family and community activities we may well be learning all the time, even if it is only about managing children or teenagers or using the latest gadget or computer software effectively.

If our work is busy or we have full domestic commitments, the last thing we may want to do is go on a one-week course. But to see development as equating to going on week-long courses is a dated notion. The best of development is rarely about sitting in a row in a lecture room. The best of development will be engaging and practical, combining workshops, individual research and practical exploration. I have found that the most effective way of developing leaders has combined three-hour workshops with focused, one-to-one coaching conversations, targeted reading, practical application and careful review.

As you begin to think about personal development, the starting point should not be: What courses do I go on? The most productive starting point is about the outcomes you want to attain in terms of competences and confidence in different contexts. Finding the right way forward comes through a combination of understanding the outcomes you want, recognizing your personal preferences, in terms of the way you learn and being realistic about the opportunities available to you. If you develop knowledge and understanding most effectively through going to lectures, go to lectures. If you learn most effectively through dialogue with others, go to interactive workshops and join learning sets. What matters is combining the approach to learning that best suits your rational brain and your emotional make-up. For learning to stick you have got to be enjoying the learning, even if it is hard work.

Deciding on the right development for you often comes through experiencing situations you are not used to. Chris was thinking about moving into teaching as a second career: he spent a couple of days sitting in on classes in a local school and talking to the teachers. These two days gave him a fascinating overview about what life as a teacher would be like. Jacqueline spent some time with a hospital chaplain, which helped her think through whether being a chaplain was something she would be good at and find fulfilling and what type of preparation she would need.

The better the quality of ongoing feedback we have from those people we trust, the easier it will be to focus our continuing personal development. If we start off each week by saying, 'This is what I am going to experiment with', we can then review at the end of the week what we have done and what has been learnt. The more we can see development as a never-ending process, the more open we will be to widening our repertoire of skills and understanding.

Bob knew that he had to become better at influencing others. He was conscious that building partnerships was increasingly important in the work he did. He observed how others built alliances. He reflected on how he had built a sense of common purpose in the past and what he had learnt from previous experiences. Bob consciously observed other people who influenced well and noted down what they did.

When Bob was meeting new people he decided to be more systematic about how he remembered their names and their interests. He then built a sense of mutual understanding over a sequence of conversations. Bob talked to a range of different people about how they sought to influence others in a way that was authentic and believable. He went on a short, one-day workshop on negotiating skills and then embedded that learning by leading some negotiating with external suppliers. Bob wanted, and ensured he got, regular feedback from senior people in the organization. He knew that he had to keep developing both his technical skills in IT and his leadership and managerial skills in a way that kept him engaged and wanting to learn.

Some points for reflection

- What type of development engages you most?
- What stopped you over the last year from receiving the development and experiences you needed?

51

- Who do you need to get on board to support the development you want to achieve?
- What are the practical outcomes you want to reach in terms of your own confidence and competences?
- Are there people you might work-shadow or talk to about their roles?
- What are your plans for your personal learning over the next six months?

12

Be ready for opportunities

Opportunities can come along like London buses. They either come in a group of two or three together or there is a long gap with no bus. Sometimes life feels devoid of opportunities. On other occasions there are a number of possibilities we want to pursue and not enough time to do all of them justice.

When we have a lot of commitments because of work, young children or elderly parents, we see opportunities to engage with different activities that we cannot take advantage of. We may be asked to be a school governor or a representative on a community group, or the possibility of some part-time work is floated past us. These are all things we would love to do but have not got the time or flexibility to be able to take on. On other occasions, when a youngster has left home or we have had to move to part-time working, we are looking for opportunities that do not appear. Either way we can be frustrated about having too many or too few opportunities.

When the children were young I often used to sit with them on the garden wall overlooking the road. We each took a colour and counted the number of cars that passed that were painted in that colour. Normally you do not notice red cars, but when you begin to look for them there are a surprising number that pass by. The moral of this story is to think through what the opportunities are that you are looking for and then be alert to them.

If you want to take up a role within the community where you live and you keep looking, opportunities almost invariably arise, such as helping edit a local magazine, becoming a junior leader of a Cub or Brownie pack, becoming a sides-person at a church or taking on a periodic responsibility to care for some elderly people.

If we are bored in the particular work we do, can we be looking out for opportunities to contribute in a different way? It might be looking out for an opportunity to do the same type of work in a different organization; for example, moving to a different hospital, business or sports club. Alternatively, it might be looking at opportunities to use your skills in a slightly different way: as a secondary school teacher you might want to work with adults, or as a nurse you might want to move from working in a hospital to becoming a community nurse. Or you may be an accountant working in a small manufacturing business and welcome the opportunity to lead the finance function in a firm of solicitors.

You may not want to move jobs and it may not be realistic to do so. But you might be looking for some complementary activities that would mean you could do your day job with a greater feeling of satisfaction. As a classroom teacher there may be an attraction in taking on a functional specialism and developing some wider curriculum that will provide variety and a new stimulus in your professional thinking.

As a doctor in a hospital you might offer to join a couple of planning committees that will give you a greater appreciation of how decisions are made, or should be made, in a hospital. Looking for wider opportunities to add to the day job might be about widening your credentials to be able to move on, or it might be to enable you to discharge your prime responsibilities well and to keep you fresh through the value of external stimulus.

Bob was surprised when a couple of his friends suggested he might stand to be a governor at his local secondary school. He could see that his IT perspective might be useful. One or two sponsors saw him as good at bringing a wider perspective and understanding of the links between the school and the community. Bob was persuaded to stand and was appointed. He soon found himself involved in a number of committees looking at different aspects of school life. Bob was surprised how much he enjoyed these responsibilities. He realized he had a valuable contribution to make.

A consequence of taking on this non-executive role was that Bob became more confident about speaking on committees within his business, having now realized that he could contribute successfully in this type of forum. Bob was not as bored at work as he had been when working on certain kinds of projects. He now had this external stimulus that kept him motivated during times when his day job was less interesting. Bob felt that both he and his employer had gained from his taking on this wider role as a school governor. He was now much more confident in contributing in a wider range of circumstances.

Some points for reflection

- Look for opportunities where you can use your skills in a way that will build your confidence in applying your gifts in a range of situations.

- Look for opportunities to contribute both outside and inside of work.
- Calibrate opportunities, assessing what you would learn and what is the practical contribution you can make.
- Look for different types of opportunities that will draw out different aspects of your character and skills.
- Seek opportunities outside work that develop your competence and confidence in a way that will benefit you at work.

PART 4

KNOW HOW YOU HANDLE DERAILERS

De-railers can come in all sorts of shapes and sizes. The unexpected can 'knock you sideways'. Knowing what derailers might hit you and thinking through how you handle them can be invaluable in enabling you to prepare for different eventualities. Sometimes, inevitably, you are caught by surprise. You had not expected your marriage to break up, or a teenager to take drugs, to lose your job or a friend to become severely injured.

It can be worth preparing how you would respond to de-railers, without being preoccupied by that prospect. You do not want to be looking forward with a gloomy perspective or else the joy in the present can be sapped. This part looks at different, potential derailers and how you might handle them. It considers when stress hurts, when family pressures pile up, when events go wrong and when your energy sags.

13

When stress hurts

You can feel caught by pressures that won't go away. Your mind might be jumping around from one topic to another with a reduced ability to focus continually on one issue. Your sleep pattern might be disturbed. You might be more irritable at home. Your family may be noticing that your voice sounds stressed, your face looks tauter than normal. They observe that you become annoyed more quickly and do not have the patience that had previously been one of your characteristics.

When stress hits us we want to fight it and suppress it. Stress is for wimps and not for us, but stress is often a reality that has to be faced up to and cannot be ignored. The sooner we face up to stress the better. Ignoring it and pretending it is not there can lead to the stress becoming worse and more insidious.

Handling a short-term stressful situation brings out the adrenalin. The type of stress that is damaging is long term and can bite into our physical and mental health, destroying routines that have become precious to us.

There is no one perfect way of addressing stress. The key ingredients in handling stress include naming it, understanding it and talking about it with trusted others. Once we name it and stop pretending it is not there, we can begin to understand it and decide how we are going to tackle it. Observing how other members of our family have handled stress can bring insights about our make-up and the patterns of reaction we are likely to go through.

Understanding the causes of the stress we face can give us prompts about how best to address them. Sometimes the answer is straightforward. If being late for a meeting causes stress, do not be late for important meetings. If a senior person can unnerve you, prepare carefully for those conversations. If guidance appears unclear to you, check out whether you have properly understood it. If a particular individual causes you stress, think through how best you handle those encounters so the chance of being derailed is reduced.

Sometimes stress can result from an excessive preoccupation with a single issue or a particular individual. A solution can be to seek the views of people we trust who will see our situation in a wider perspective. Progress might come from doing something entirely different (such as engaging in intense, physical activity), becoming immersed in an entirely different personal interest or reading books that engage our imagination and take us into very different thought processes.

Most people have been through periods of stress. Recalling how we handled these previously can remind us what is likely to enable us to handle current or future stress acceptably well. But where the symptoms of stress are acute, medical help is essential and not just desirable. For some a short break away from work, or a programme of CBT (cognitive behavioural therapy), can enable a new start.

For others, living with a degree of depression is a fact of life. For them, recognizing the patterns and knowing how to minimize the effect of periods of depression is important in maintaining equilibrium at home and at work. The person who understands the patterns of when they are at risk of a dip has developed a way of making progress when their wellbeing is good, and recognizing that at low times they have to focus on the essentials and leave desirables for another time.

Stress can feel humiliating. Why should I suffer when others don't? But living with stress can be equated with living with different types of disability, such as poor hearing or limited eyesight. Handling the disability thoughtfully can restrict its impact. It can also enable you to understand and work effectively with those who might have similar characteristics.

Linda had been the head of department at a sixth-form college. She enjoyed working with the students and got satisfaction out of planning the organization of work in the college. The other staff regularly sought her advice and regarded her as a source of wisdom and authority. But Linda found it stressful being a leader in the college and a classroom teacher. She felt at everyone's beck and call. She could become tired and exhausted. She always tried to be patient at college but her family knew when she was getting stressed.

Linda knew that part of the way of handling her stress was to plan carefully. She knew there was a risk of her being overconscientious. She needed to be clear in her own mind when some activities could wait. Talking through some of her conflicting priorities with others helped her put them in perspective and reduce her stress. Visits to her mother, a perpetual optimist, cheered her up. Participation in her church community helped her to enjoy the company of others without feeling she had to be in a leadership role. Linda recognized that coping with the ups and downs of stress was part of being a head of department. She accepted the cycle she would go through each term, but told herself it was worth it because making a difference to students' lives as a college lecturer was very important to her.

Some points for reflection

- When stress hurts, observe what is happening and seek to understand why.
- Remember how you have handled periods of stress before.
- See what aspects of life can be de-stressed.
- Have a plan and seek to stick to it.
- Recognize that living with stress is part of life.

14

When family pressures pile up

Mid-life can be anywhere from the ages thirty-five to seventy. Family pressures can range from demanding children to wayward siblings or parents with declining health. We feel we can cope well with one type of family pressure. It becomes more complicated when they are cumulative. It is a delight to have a grandparent who can look after the four year old or pick up the eight year old from school. But as the grandparent becomes more elderly we can become apprehensive about leaving the grandchild in their care. We worry what might happen when they become forgetful.

We enjoy time with the children but worry about their education and the company they might keep. As they enter their teenage years we are conscious that our control on the influences upon them becomes increasingly limited.

The children might be engaged in activities that involve a lot of ferrying. We can become frustrated that acting as a chauffeur is taking up so much time. The children want to be involved in midweek activities, which means that one of the parents has to be available to choreograph these movements. As a parent you love the children, your siblings and your parents dearly, but in combination the pressures can feel relentless. The result can be a strong sensation of 'there is no time for me'. At this point fantasy can take over, with alcohol or even soft drugs an attraction that previously would not have been countenanced.

Perhaps the best way to address family pressures is to be explicit about what the family commitments are and how they might be prioritized. Which of your family members are dependent upon you and how much do you want to accept that dependency? How can you enable elderly parents to be as independent as possible and be there for key moments when they do need your practical support? How best do you equip your children to grow in confidence and independence so they are able, over time, to make their own decisions?

With siblings, friends and godchildren, where do you draw the boundary between what is essential and what is desirable? Sometimes hard choices have to be made, which means you are not able to give as much time to some people as you would have wished. Perhaps the answer is about quality of time rather than quantity of time. Skype or Facetime can be wonderful ways of keeping in touch with people when travel time to visit them needs to be deployed for other commitments.

For some people, going to work is a wonderful way to put family pressures into perspective. It takes you out of the house into a very different realm. When family pressures are emotionally acute, training yourself to focus wholeheartedly on work can enable you to withstand the debilitating consequences that can come from family pressures.

An immediate response to family pressures can be, 'How do I reduce the demands at work?' But increasing the interest and engagement at work can give you the intellectual satisfaction that enables you to cope more effectively with some of the emotional pressures at home. There is a delicate balance between increasing your engagement at work in a constructive way, and using emotion in work as an avoidance of family pressures.

When family pressures do build up, reminding yourself of the importance of family life and the joy that comes from family activities is important so that family life overall remains positive and not debilitating.

Linda was conscious that life was a balancing act between her work, her two young children, her husband, her mother and her sister. She knew that quality time with her children was vital. She visited her mum once a week and Skyped her sister once a fortnight. Family holidays were important in keeping an equilibrium at home. Planning family holidays was a treat that her children and her husband enjoyed. The pleasure was as much in the anticipation as in the reality. When family pressures were acute a routine that worked well was time spent thinking about the next holiday or sharing photographs of a previous holiday.

Linda knew that she was dependent upon her mother for emergency childcare. She knew that she could not rely on this in perpetuity. Linda began to use an alternative solution in emergencies. She knew that she had to have different ways of handling emergencies going forward. She knew she had periodically to be able to allocate time to spend with her sister, who had lost her job, and planned that time carefully. There was a risk that what came last was the relationship with her husband. Thankfully they were able to talk this through and knew when the point was reached that they needed for their own wellbeing to go out for a 'dinner date'.

Some points for reflection

- When family pressures pile up, remind yourself how important family life is to you.
- Plan how best to allocate your time to different family members.

- Be open in talking through the different pressures and how best to communicate with each member of the family.
- Focus on quality rather than quantity time.
- Use modern technology efficiently in ensuring the best type of communication with family members, which encourages them and you.

15

When events go wrong

The phrase 'events dear boy' was attributed to Harold
Macmillan, Britain's Prime Minister from 1957 to 1963.
We can have carefully laid plans but there will always be
'events' that are unexpected and take us off course. Perhaps we
had anticipated succeeding our boss but the business is taken
over and the new owners are looking for a different type of
manager. We had anticipated staying in the current school as
a senior member of staff until we retired but the numbers of
pupils have dropped and there is likely to be a merger with
another school, which will mean our job is at risk.

We might have worked in a successful small business, but
suddenly the product it manufactures is no longer sought after.
Or the organization where you work that produces software
has seen the market drop because a better quality product is
now available from overseas.

We might have been working on a particular project that,
through no fault of our own, is late or not up to standard, and
the contract is terminated. Because of public expenditure cuts
the future of the battalion is at risk and the long sought for
promotion is probably never going to happen.

Sometimes a piece of work we are involved in does not reach
the desired standard and we are partially culpable. We have
to live with a blemish on our CV and have a very good explanation about what we learnt and how we have moved on. We
may have had no direct responsibility for what went wrong but

have to live with the consequences. It is little comfort that we are not directly responsible.

How best do we live with the consequences? A first step is understanding the facts and being able to give a clear explanation to ourselves and others about what went wrong and why. Once we have accepted the reality of our situation, the next step is being clear about what we have learnt both from observing others and about our own contribution, attitude and impact. Part of the learning is reflecting on how we would react in a similar situation if it happened again. Sometimes we will be able to identify how we would plan it differently in future. On other occasions the honest answer is that we would not have responded in a different way.

When events go wrong we have to 'dust ourselves off' and recognize our emotional reactions and then move on. Part of a forward look is acknowledging how quickly the events of the past can be put behind you. There will always be a legacy in your own mind, but time passes and there are new people and different expectations. Reputations can be rebuilt even if you feel tainted by something that has gone wrong in the past.

Sometimes it can help to turn physically around and face, metaphorically, an event that went wrong, and then turn through 180 degrees to look at the future, deliberately stepping forward and leaving the events of the past behind you. When significant relationships go wrong, the practical steps might be to be honest about the facts, face up to the events of the past, recognize your learning and then look forward and step into the future better equipped, wiser and more realistic.

Linda was very proud of her college and talked glowingly about its success in the education of a range of different pupils. Much to her surprise an inspection report was more critical than she had expected and raised some questions about the effectiveness of the leadership. At a similar time her eldest child began to get equivocal reports from her school. Linda was conscious that a couple of things in her life were going wrong at the same time.

Linda's first inclination was to go into a 'try harder' mode in terms of what she did at work and in terms of how she pressed her daughter to make the most of school. Linda's husband gave her some good advice to slow down and reflect on why these two situations had arisen. Linda recognized that she had been missing some key signs at college about two or three members of staff not being fully on board with her approach. But she also recognized that certain of her daughter's friendships were going through rocky periods, which probably meant she was not so motivated at school.

Linda recognized that she needed to adapt her approach and be more sensitive to the needs of some of her lecturer colleagues, and to be less 'pushy' as a parent with her daughter. Linda accepted that the problem was partially because she was blinkered and not observing fully what was going on. She also reminded herself that things will always be going wrong and that she would be less thrown by these situations if she could take them in her stride a little more readily.

Some points for reflection

- When things go wrong, remember that is how life works.
- When one part of life is not going so well, sit that alongside other parts of life that are feeling more positive.

- Always focus on what you are learning from these situations and how they prepare you for the future.
- Remember that good can come out of any situation where there is a willingness to learn and move on.

16

When your energy sags

In your twenties your energy seems never ending. In your thirties you have learnt to harness that energy in a more measured way. By your forties your energy levels may go up and down. By your fifties your energy levels may vary markedly depending on how captivated you are by the activity you are engaged in.

When your energy sags, your first response may be that you need a good sleep, some physical exercise or to switch your brain into a totally different activity.

When something catches your imagination your weariness can go as quickly as it came. When your curiosity is sparked it is as if the engines are firing up and you are ready to listen and learn in a fresh way. When we see our imagination caught and observe a new freshness in us, this enthusiasm can spill over into other areas of life. When you light one corner of a bonfire it quickly spreads across the whole structure. If we can light some enthusiasm in one part of our lives then it is quite likely to spread through the other parts.

Starting a new friendship can remind us that we have interesting things to contribute to conversations. Developing a new interest reminds us that our brain is able to learn new things and be excited by new experiences. Learning how to use the next generation of information technology reassures us that we are not as dumb as we had previously thought. Reconnecting with people through social networking can remind us that we have expertise and experience we can share.

When our energy sags over an extended period it is a warning that adjustments in our attitudes and our lifestyle may be needed. Our levels of energy may well be a barometer of how we are feeling about life and not just a measure of our physical fitness. My energy levels in my mid-sixties are higher than they were twenty years ago. This is partly because I enjoy the work I do now more than the work I did twenty years ago. But I am also more comfortable about how the different aspects of my life fit together. Having grandchildren makes you feel younger – well, most of the time!

When your energy sags, part of the response might be recognizing that you are growing older and do not have the same levels of physical energy. But it can also be worth reflecting on what activities will renew your energy: perhaps it is following a new interest or taking an existing interest to another level. Perhaps it is consciously choosing an attitude of mind that tries to move out of your thinking the sagging hopes, despondency or defeatism that drags you down and sucks the energy and life out of you. Can you squeeze to one side some of the negativity so you can see that there is a way forward?

It might be worth thinking what will jolt you into thinking more positively about the future and bring more energy to moving forward. For me listening to brass-band music or barn-dance music lifts my spirits and raises my desire to take an idea forward. Going for long-distance walks covering seventy miles in a week clears my head and enables me to work through what are the next challenges to address and how best I am going to tackle them in a way that is sustainable.

I encourage you to go on a very personal journey, reflecting on your energy levels and what type of freshness and new experiences or new interests will rekindle energy and curiosity in you so that your energy grows and does not diminish with age.

Linda was exhausted at the end of each college term but by the end of each holiday was 'up and running' and ready to tackle a new term. With each new generation of children she was reminded why she came into teaching and what kept her so engaged in her work. After five years as a head of department she began to reflect on whether the energy in the role would sag after a while. She concluded that she did not want the additional responsibility of being a deputy principal and that there was no particular advantage in moving colleges.

But Linda also recognized that she needed to keep fresh. She decided to do some professional updating courses and to join a choir. She had always loved singing and concluded that being part of a choir again would rekindle her interest in music and allow her to be part of a very different type of community. Enjoying the discipline of choral singing reminded her how much she enjoyed this type of activity. The pleasure of the singing infused the rest of her life and ensured that she got even more pleasure out of the lecturing job.

Some points for reflection

- When your energy sags, remind yourself what gives you most energy and make time to do that activity.
- Reflect on what might give you a freshness and a new energy and think about what new activities you can do or re-engage with.
- Remember that pacing your energy will be important however energized you might feel now.
- Reflect on what activities will give you freshness that can spin off into the rest of your life.

REBALANCE

PART 5

STAY PROFESSIONAL AND FOCUSED

Perhaps you know what matters most to you. You feel as if you are going in the right direction and then you feel a bit stuck. You do not want to rush into work every morning. There are pressures at home that are building up. It feels like an uphill climb. Things you used to take in your stride can feel daunting.

It feels a bit tough when there is a financial squeeze or you go through a rough patch. It can feel deflating when others overtake you. Sometimes you can feel a victim and caught in a trap and unable to move forward. In these situations your rational brain tells you to stay professional and focused. Emotionally it is not always that straightforward.

17

When there is a financial squeeze

You have taken pride in living within your financial means and have not accumulated debt. Sound advice had been to pay off the credit-card bill every month, and you have normally managed to do that. A significant part of your monthly income goes into either paying rent or making mortgage payments. You don't particularly want to think about the consequences of a rise in mortgage interest rates.

Financially you are living within your means, just. You are assuming your pay will gradually increase. But the experience of recent years has been little or no pay increases alongside a relentless, if modest, increase in prices.

You can be preoccupied with thinking about the consequences of high energy bills, more costly food, the expectations from children for new clothes and toys. There can be a spiral of rising expectations that look as if they could soak up more resources than are likely to be available. Maybe you will inherit some money one day, but that is a long time off, especially as parents are living longer and are likely to incur significantly more costs covering their care as they get older.

Your immediate response might be to work longer hours and to go for promotion in order to increase your income. That might be the right answer provided it does not sap your energy too much and undermine the other priorities that are of particular importance for you. Perhaps it is time to rationalize some of your expenditure. What can be recycled or bought second-hand? Might clothes be worn for longer, the heating dropped a couple of degrees or more modest cuts of meat bought? Perhaps holidays could be in a cottage or under canvas rather than in a hotel.

Perhaps using money more economically, rather than being a hardship, can be a satisfying exercise. Even frugality can become fun provided the basics of food and shelter are covered.

At a time when you feel your finances are squeezed it might be a good moment to review how much you give away. Paradoxically, when resources feel tight might be a cathartic moment to give more away to charities you support. Giving money to an aid project or to a local church for its work with the disadvantaged or with young people can put your own financial circumstances into a different light. We may feel financially hard done by, but giving to others in greater need can bring home that our reality is not as severe as we think in our dark moments.

It may be that we have lived on the edge and not built up any savings. We have wanted to do the best for our children and saving for a rainy day has hardly seemed a priority. When financial reality hits home, our past foolhardiness can seem almost tragic. Your response might be 'Never again will I leave myself without a financial cushion after I begin earning again.'

A financial squeeze can lead to uncharacteristic behaviours and anger against ourselves or others, or excessive generosity to try to demonstrate to the rest of the world that all is well. When money is tight what is needed is a combination of careful planning, a cool head and a measured approach that cuts out non-essentials, while spending the money that is available on the priorities that keep the family together.

When there is a financial squeeze, facing squarely up to reality is important. Too often there can be a pretence that there is no problem. Keeping up appearances can waste precious resources for too long. Money spent can never be spent again. Facing reality, doing sums and making conscious and deliberate decisions can take the fear out of financial uncertainty and make the future bearable.

Steve had been a vicar for three years. His wife Sandra had taught and their combined income was enough to live on and save a little. When their first child was born, Sandra decided not to go back to work. She had found teaching very time-demanding and could not see how she could readily be a good mum and a full-time teacher. When the maternity pay ended Steve and Sandra found it tough. Their expenditure was about the same as their income for the first few months. But then the car needed some major repairs. They wanted to go away on holiday. There were presents to buy. There were no funds available for these 'luxuries' so they had to use their savings.

Steve and Sandra decided that they needed a conscious plan about economizing. They dropped the temperature of the heating by a couple of degrees and wore thicker sweaters in the house. They stopped buying new clothes for their baby and were happy to receive handed-down clothes from others. They arranged a couple of holidays through doing house swaps with friends. They increased their giving to an overseas charity they supported. They graciously accepted hospitality when they were offered weekends away in other people's homes. Once they had got used to using money in a different way they were reasonably content with this new equilibrium. They recognized that one day Sandra would go back to work and they could build up their savings again, but as a vicar Steve knew that he would never be well off. That had been his choice and he was happy to live with it, well most of the time.

Some points for reflection

- What is the financial reality you need to face up to?
- How best can you plan to use your financial resources well?
- What do you need to try and save for, for the future?
- What choices can you make that will enable you to better use the resources you have available?

18

When you go through a rough patch

Life is rarely always a bed of roses. In reality, sitting in a bed of roses for a long period can be boring and painful, especially if you sit on a rose thorn. Life may be going well one day and not so well the next. You may be the flavour of the month for one period and then appear to be able to do nothing right for the next. You are the same person bringing the same attitudes and values and yet you can be hailed as the saviour of the organization one month and a spent force the next.

For a period we may feel full of optimism. No problem is insurmountable. Whatever the obstacle we can identify a way through. We bring a positive approach that others want to follow, but in another period every small problem can feel huge. Instead of scampering up the mountain we are struggling step by step on a rough pathway. What was once joyous can feel relentlessly difficult. It is a rough patch that appears to be going on and on.

For a period we have been able to sit lightly to a few critical comments. We shrug our shoulders and move on, but on other occasions any slightly critical comment hits home and pierces our self-confidence. Our energy disappears and we feel worn down and stuck. When we go through a rough patch it can be helpful to look back over the journey we have made. Remembering how we have overcome past problems can help us to renew our strength for the future. Having a dossier of positive comments people have made about us can lift our spirits, if we allow ourselves to re-read those comments and believe them.

Going through a rough patch can involve keeping pushing forward step by step in a focused and determined way, and when the squall arrives, putting on a coat and waterproof that protect us. Keeping in our mind the destination can give us the courage to keep going through the wind and the rain even though it feels relentless.

As you go through a dark forest on a pathway that is unclear, what keeps you going is the belief that the forest will end and that there will be a way out on the other side. As a leader there will be moments when it feels like going through a dark forest. Resilience comes through believing that there will be a way out the other side and that you have the capacity to reach that destination. Progress comes through planning carefully, taking one step at a time, bringing people with you, explaining your intent and building the support or at least the acquiescence of others.

There may be a need to change direction. It is about finding ways of keeping going and not letting emotional reactions undermine your resolve to find a new route through and reach a better place where you can find more of an equilibrium.

Steve had been well received when he started in his parish. The honeymoon period seemed to go on for two to three years. He could do no wrong and the parishioners welcomed the great majority of his ideas. He thought this harmony would go on for ever. Steve wanted to initiate a building project and met more opposition than he had expected. There was grumbling about his not fully understanding the community. Suddenly there appeared to be a scepticism in the air about his ideas.

Steve was initially deflated, but then recognized that he was reacting emotionally to the concerns of some of the parishioners. He sat down with those who were hesitant about the building project and better understood their concern. But the criticism had affected his confidence. He had been working too hard and was too emotionally dependent on praise from members of the church. He knew he had to stand back more, and ensured he took his holidays so that he could put his work in the parish into a wider perspective.

Steve came out of his rough patch with his confidence restored, recognizing that this was probably an inevitable process. He felt stronger and more able to be philosophical when there were critical comments about some of his ideas. He had built stronger bridges with the range of people in his congregation and was able to plan more effectively for the future.

Some points for reflection

- Remember when you go through a rough patch how you have handled such situations before.
- Do not forget the good things that are happening that are sources of encouragement.
- See the good that is coming out of the difficulties, even if that is just about your building up your resilience.
- Seek to have a plan for moving forward and keep going step by step, noting the progress you are making.

19

When others overtake you

You have enjoyed the work you do. You have had a track record of success. Lots of people have spoken well of your contribution. For a number of years you felt as if you were riding on the crest of a wave. You moved successfully from one post to another. You worked with different groups of clients, customers, patients or pupils and had a sequence of good performance reviews. It felt like ever onwards and upwards.

And then a colleague overtakes you. You go for a promotion and feel you have strong credentials, yet it is somebody else who gets the job. The first time this happens you shrug your shoulders and say the decision was all about personal preference and whether your approach fitted in a particular context or not. You are not too downhearted. The second time it happens you are able to bring into play the same set of explanations. But by the third time you are passed over for a promotion there is recognition that there is a pattern here.

Perhaps the moment when stark reality hits home is when someone who used to work for you now becomes your boss. That is a moment of truth when you realize you are not going to reach the top of the organization. When someone overtakes you the rational brain can often see the reasons why and their attributes that have warranted their elevation. Your emotional reaction might be one of pique or frustration. The phrase 'It is not fair' is in your mind if not on your lips. You want to protest about the injustice, but equally you know that you have to work effectively with your new boss and not let your frustrations show or undermine your approach.

When someone does overtake you a first step is to be as rational as possible about what has happened. As you note down the reasons and understand the circumstances you can more readily accept what has happened and live with it. Accepting the inevitable involves understanding your emotional reactions and sitting outside them, so you can more readily live with the disappointment when you see your peers or those younger than you promoted above you.

Part of the acceptance of the elevation of others comes through your accepting that the other person is better suited to the more senior role, or that you have a balance of life that is more compatible with your priorities and preferences. Seeing someone promoted above you can initially produce a reaction of disappointment. Having thought it through, you might become relieved that you had not been promoted and can be more accepting of the position you are currently in.

The fact that someone overtakes you might give you the jolt you needed. Perhaps you had become too complacent and set in your ways. Now might be the time to think again about whether your approach to your current work needs to become fresher and more energetic. Or the jolt might mean now is the time to think about other options and look to move to another post or into a slightly different sphere.

This might be the jolt you need to think about a radically different career choice. When someone does overtake you it is important to watch that you do not spiral into feeling a sense of failure. It is important to remind yourself about what you have delivered and achieved and not feel as if the world is coming to an end because someone else has been promoted.

Steve enjoyed the independence of being a vicar. He knew he had the support of the archdeacon who had responsibility for the county area. He was on good terms with his colleagues in the area. When the post of area dean became available he informed the archdeacon that he would be interested in taking on this coordinating role for the local area. To his slight surprise someone else was appointed.

Steve's initial reaction was one of disappointment, although he recognized that ambition was not the type of behaviour it was appropriate to exhibit. When he asked the archdeacon about whether he had been considered as a potential candidate, the archdeacon thoughtfully explained that the colleague who had been appointed had more time for this additional role and was ideally equipped to handle some forthcoming reorganization proposals.

The archdeacon sensed a slight disappointment in Steve's tone of voice and stressed that there were no negative reasons about Steve that had led to his not being appointed. He subsequently asked Steve to take on a couple of responsibilities across part of the diocese that gave him the broader understanding and experience that he was seeking. Steve recognized that the archdeacon had handled his disappointment well. The outcome was a better outcome for Steve than being appointed area dean as someone else had to deal with some difficult problems that Steve would not have relished tackling.

Some points for reflection

- Congratulate those who overtake you genuinely and warmly.

- Seek to understand the reasons why they have been appointed and not you.
- Sit lightly to your emotional reactions and work them through.
- Think through the beneficial consequences of not being appointed.
- Believe that good will come out of the situation that has caused you disappointment.

20

When you feel a victim

The business in which you work has been taken over. The role you do is already done in head office and you are likely to be made redundant. Your first reaction is to sulk, look very unhappy or protest. The more aggrieved or unhappy you look the more likely you are to lose your job. Perhaps your job is going to go anyway. But perhaps if you thought through how you might contribute to the organization in a slightly different way going forward, then your redundancy might not be inevitable.

When someone feels a victim they are quite likely to be a victim. The person who feels a victim will inevitably be giving that impression to others. The emotional reaction that comes with feeling a victim is not something that commends itself to others. Sympathy and warmth might ebb away quite quickly.

It is easy to slip into victim mode if redundancies are mooted and cut-backs seen as inevitable. The fear of redundancy can become a self-fulfilling prophecy if your demeanour looks negative, unco-operative and pessimistic.

The risk of going into victim mode is that you feel comfortable in that mode. Being a victim enables you to have an explanation for your misfortunes. The risk is that you wallow in your misfortunes and then have a ready-made excuse for not breaking out of your despondency.

Being in victim mode can be like being stuck in a vice where the handle is tightening the grip. Breaking out of victim mode can require decisive action. It can be physically important to move out of the space where you feel a victim so you are liberated from its claws. Breaking out from being a victim can require bold repetition of the phrase, 'I am not going to allow myself to be a victim.' It might mean walking briskly with a trusted friend and talking through your reactions. It will mean working it through to the point where you can smile at yourself and the way you have been 'in the grip' of an emotional reaction.

Sometimes we are victims of circumstances. Sometimes we have to pick ourselves up, dust ourselves down and move on. Sometimes we feel like a victim when other people do not think such a reaction is justifiable. When you feel like a victim it can often be worth talking through your reaction with others you trust to see whether your reaction is based on fact or fantasy. If feeling a victim gives you the inner resolve to burst out of constraints, then your emotional reaction has had a beneficial outcome. But that perspective can be fraught with danger if allowing yourself to feel a victim to give you energy leads to an over-aggressive response.

Perhaps the best way forward is to be able to smile at yourself and say, 'I am beginning to feel like a victim, and how do I break out of that?' Sitting lightly to the sensation of being a victim is the best way of breaking out of the strictures that victim mode can bring.

Steve had a six-month period when he was exceptionally busy. His curate had moved on and another one was not going to be in post for another year. One of the non-stipendiary ministers was doing less at the church. Steve thought that the expectations on him were rising while his resources were declining. He began to feel caught in the parish and a bit of a victim. Everyone was expecting him to solve every problem without showing a huge amount of appreciation.

Steve began to realize that he was in danger of sinking into victim mentality. On a couple of days off he went for a brisk, three-hour cycle ride. This physical exertion made him feel much better about himself and his situation. He talked through his reaction with a trusted friend and recognized what had set off in him this feeling of being a victim. Once he understood what was happening to him he knew he would be better able to handle a similar reaction next time it occured.

Some points for reflection

- When you begin to feel a victim, seek to understand the reasons for your reaction.
- Recognize the pattern of your emotional reactions.
- Seek to move into a different space to observe and understand how you are reacting.
- Talk to one or two trusted others to help you move through the victim reaction quickly.

PART 6

EMBRACE SIMPLICITY

Life seems to become ever more complicated. We are over loaded with information. I recently joined a couple of social networking sites and have been deluged with information about people's activities and seem to be connected to a huge number of people. It is fascinating to learn more about a range of places and people, but my brain can only cope with a limited amount of information at any one time. As we grow older our brains become fuller and fuller and we wonder how much more information we can handle.

This part is about the importance of embracing simplicity. Its chapters deal with de-cluttering, de-complicating, de-mystifying and de-toxing. Sometimes we have to say 'enough is enough' and it is time to focus on the essentials and be clear what is most important and what can be ignored, forgotten or dismissed.

21

De-clutter

It is only when you move house that you realize how much clutter you have collected. We cease to wear a particular piece of clothing and it sits in the wardrobe ignored and unloved, taking up space. The pair of comfortable shoes that now let in the rain we still keep because they might come in useful on a dry, summer's day. The newspaper article we thought we might read again sits in a pile becoming frayed at the edges. There is something quite comforting about still having old clothes that we might, one day, wear again.

When you go on holiday and have to keep the baggage to a minimum it is amazing how little you need to take with you. The thought of paying to take an extra bag on an air flight can trump the desire to take frivolous items with us. When I do long-distance walks and carry a backpack I have every incentive to take with me a very small number of essential items.

There are moments when our lives need de-cluttering. Perhaps there are some activities we engage with in a half-hearted way where we need to be fully engaged or to drop the connection. Perhaps we are on a mailing list for innumerable good causes and charities. Now is the moment to decide which ones we have a particular interest in and drop the connection with the myriad other good causes.

We have enjoyed taking a partial interest in a wide range of different subjects. The consequence can be that we know a little about a lot of subjects. Perhaps the time has come to decide where our primary interest lies.

When our brains feel cluttered it can be much more difficult to focus on one subject at a time. The risk is that at work we keep reflecting on family issues, or when we are at home considerations about work keep popping up in our minds. An element of de-cluttering is to focus on one subject at a time so that we are not subject to noisy interference that can easily disturb our equilibrium.

When I moved into executive coaching work, a skill I needed to develop was to concentrate entirely on one person at a time. To be effective as a coach I needed to give someone sole, undivided attention and be able to block out thinking about any other subject. The consequence of training myself to focus on one person or one subject at a time has meant that I am much less able to multi-task. On balance, training myself to focus on one person or subject at a time, so that clutter is blocked out, has been an advantage and not a disadvantage.

Sometimes we can be cluttered with emotional reactions from the past when it is time to leave those reactions behind. Asking ourselves the explicit question, 'What are the emotional reactions that are dated and need to be left behind?' can help us focus on how we need to move on. Maybe there is resentment about someone else's success, anger about the way we have been treated or a 'chip on the shoulder' about what happened to us in our youth that needs to be named and discarded. Cluttered emotions can blur our forward vision and mean that we feel stuck. As soon as we move the clutter of redundant emotions we can often see a way ahead more clearly and recognize that we can break out of fears and constraints that have held us back.

Marcia was head of a laboratory in a pharmaceutical business. She was a mum with two children aged twelve and fourteen. Her husband was also in a busy job. Marcia's life was full. She loved to keep in touch with a range of different friends. She organized her life by having long lists but she was always running late and regularly disappointed with herself because she never got more than halfway down the list of tasks she had set herself. Marcia felt guilty that she did not lead her laboratory as well as she would have liked. There were always other pressures. She found it very difficult to focus on issues at the laboratory beyond the immediate. She prided herself on being able to multi-task but recognized that multi-tasking meant a lot of things were done in part, in a way that did not fully satisfy her.

Marcia reluctantly recognized that life was too cluttered. For her own sanity, and for the good of her career and her family, she needed to simplify her life. The starting point was reducing the interference so that when she was leading the laboratory she was not focusing on forthcoming family conversations. Marcia taught herself to be more single-minded and more willing to jettison irrelevant thoughts. She became more willing to park issues until the right time came to deal with them, through being more disciplined about when she should be single-minded and when she should multi-think or multi-task.

Some points for reflection

- What should you throw out, discard and ignore in order to de-clutter?
- What can you stop receiving information on or seeking information about?
- What emotional reactions might be discarded as historic and irrelevant?

- How might you train your brain to focus on one theme at a time with a reduction in interference from other areas?
- What type of bonfire of historic attitudes might you light so that you become less cluttered?

22

De-complicate

De-cluttering is about removing baggage from the past and reducing the interference that limits our effectiveness as a leader at work, in the community and within our family. Decomplicating is about looking forward at our priorities and trying to be clear what matters most to us. As we look forward our first reaction is often that we have very little freedom. We are constrained in lots of ways. The opportunity to make a difference is limited because of the range of responsibilities we have. But how much can we simplify our aspirations so that they become more attainable.

We might be partly involved in a church. We do not want to become too involved or life will become too complicated and the expectations upon us will be more than we are able to handle. We do not want to disappoint other people or ourselves so we do not want to put ourselves in situations where there will be expectations upon us that we cannot meet. One approach to being involved in a church is to be very clear on the limits of that involvement. You might say that you will either teach in junior church twice a month or assist with giving a lift to an elderly person twice a month, but limit your involvement at that point.

You might want to be involved in the school where your children are educated, but realistically you decide to limit that involvement to a couple of activities. Far better for you to be involved in a limited number of activities and do them well than feel half-hearted and unsatisfied in doing a wider range of tasks.

De-complicating at work might be about readjusting your aspirations. It might be about accepting that you will never be the chief executive. Your sense of ambition may need to be refocused and more realistic. Seeing your ceiling as one level above where you are rather than five levels above can help bring a realism that de-complicates your life. If your aspiration is one level higher, then that can provide a clearer rationale for your choice of activities in your current role.

De-complicating can involve being clearer about what is the impact you want to have. A natural tendency might be to want to solve all the problems in an organization. If we are more focused on the difference we think we can make, then the actions we want to take are not likely to be as complicated.

When we see younger people full of ideas and energy our first reaction might be one of weariness or inadequacy. But what we can bring after a number of years of experience is the capacity to ask good questions and the ability to identify essential next steps. Enabling those with energy and enthusiasm to identify key next steps they need to take is a significant contribution to practical progress. If we can help others to de-complicate issues, we can feel a personal satisfaction about our contribution that helps simplify and clarify.

As an experienced leader, a significant gift you can bring to others is to seek to de-complicate issues and identify what are the key considerations and ways of taking action forward.

Marcia knew that she had to de-complicate some of the processes in the laboratory, which was too willing to take on short-term assignments from other scientists. Marcia knew that the laboratory had to allocate more

*time for planning ahead and be better at prioritizing
the assignments it was willing to take on. Marcia was
trying to be too accommodating.*

*Marcia agreed with her assistants how they would
differentiate between different requests. She had conversations with different clients so there was better forward
planning. With clearer planning and better priorities the
work of the laboratory seemed less complicated. Marcia
decided that she needed to bring the same approach into
her family life. She talked with her daughters in more
detail about what activities they particularly wanted
to be engaged in so weekends could be planned more
effectively, with less last-minute rushing around. Marcia planned her involvement in church more discrimi-
natingly by saying that she would act as a welcomer
twice a month and would join a Lent group, but would
not be part of one of the church's smaller groups during
the rest of the year.*

Some points for reflection

- Where have your priorities become too complicated and
  need to be simplified?
- How can experience of de-complicating in one area of
  life be applied in another?
- How might more planning ahead reduce some of the
  complications in your day-to-day life?
- If you simplified your priorities and were more realistic about them, how much more straightforward would
  your life be?

23

De-mystify

I was brought up by the sea in a small Yorkshire town. Sometimes the sea mist would hang over the sea and then disappear as quickly as it arrived. When you walk up a hill you can begin in clear air and then pass through a belt of mist before coming out on the other side into clearer visibility. When the mist comes down and visibility is reduced it can feel quite scary as you walk up a steep hill. But when you know the path and can follow it a step at a time, you know your destination will be reachable.

When you are in unknown territory and the mist comes down, discretion is the better part of valour and waiting for the mist to clear is better than pressing on regardless. When you stand still waiting for the mist to clear it can be cold and damp. You know the mist will go and good visibility will return after a period.

In your work you may well feel stuck in the mist. Visibility about the future is unclear; it feels cold, damp and cheerless. You feel insecure about moving from the spot where you are standing. Sometimes you just have to wait for the mist to clear. There is nothing you can do about bringing clarity to the future because of economic or political uncertainties. When the car windscreen mists up it is possible to clear the windscreen through wiping the windscreen or turning on the heater. In this example it is possible to clear the mist and see forward more sharply. When the future looks misty, sometimes we just have to wait; on other occasions we can reduce the mistiness. When our glasses mist up, it is up to us to clear them.

Sometimes de-mystifying the future is about asking some clear questions. If I aspire to doing another senior job in a different organization, asking experienced people about what I need to add to my CV is a necessary step in seeking to turn aspirations into reality.

Sometimes the mist is of our own making. Perhaps we do not want the future to become clearer because we might become disappointed about what we learn. But it can help to know that a particular avenue is closed off or that a promotion is unlikely to happen. Then we can plan more realistically for the type of role we might be able to fulfil in the future.

We might recognize for the first time that the type of role we are currently fulfilling is likely to be what we are going to be doing for the foreseeable future. De-mystifying can be about recognizing certain inevitabilities and that we need to accept our current reality and live with it.

It can be worth asking yourself whether you feel caught in the mist and cannot see the future. How much of the mist is completely outside your control and how much can you wipe away? You might say to yourself that you do need to be clear about where possible opportunities might lie. But you might also conclude that you have to live with, and are content to live with, aspects of mistiness that are not going to become clear in the foreseeable future.

Marcia enjoyed leading her laboratory but felt uncertain about the future. She was not clear whether the laboratory was likely still to exist a few years on from now. Half of her was content to live with this uncertainty because she did not want to hear that the future of the laboratory was in any way uncertain. But the other half of her wanted more clarity so she could plan her career ahead.

*When Marcia's boss moved on, Marcia had the oppor-
tunity to spend time with the research director of the
pharmaceutical company. This gave her the opportunity to ask him about the likely future of the laboratory. He shared different thoughts with Marcia about
product development. They agreed that while the laboratory's future looked clear for the next two to three
years, it would be helpful if Marcia widened her expertise so she could take on the leadership of the different
type of laboratory required in the years to come. Marcia
was glad she had taken the opportunity to ask questions about the future. The response from the research
director had de-mystified the future and had opened up
another opportunity if she was happy to do some further training and development.*

Some points for reflection

- What looks misty about the future and how much of
  that is dictated by external circumstances?
- How much do you want to remove some of the mistiness,
  or are you content living with a degree of uncertainty?
- To whom might you direct questions that will lead to a
  bit more clarity?
- If you try to de-mystify the future, how ready are you
  to live with some of the responses that might not be
  entirely to your liking?
- If the future looks misty, what are the practical, forward steps it is realistic and safe to take?

24

De-tox

Toxic gas can be poisonous and bring destruction for years to come. My elder son recently visited Chernobyl and was taken aback by the devastation that continues in that region from the fallout caused by the nuclear reactor disaster of 1986.

Sometimes toxic gases can be odourless. We do not realize we are inhaling the poison until after we begin to experience its ill effects. Because of an organization's politics or history, relationships can be toxic, with the risk of minor explosions at any moment. The poisonous gases can seep into any crack and destroy trust in working relationships or lead to a sense of suspicion that undermines co-operative working and shared endeavour.

Leaders in any organization can valuably ask the question, 'What are the toxic emotions in this organization that need to be handled with great care?' If as a leader you can identify what can be toxic within an organization and put in processes that will handle that risk, then you can have a profound effect on the sustainability of that organization.

It is worth asking yourself when you need to de-tox. What are the emotions in you that can be poisonous? When might resentment or anger erupt in you? You might have trained yourself not to show anger or resentment, but their active suppression is likely to distort the objectivity of your reaction. So much energy is likely to go into controlling the anger or resentment that the energy left to make constructive progress is much reduced.

What sets off an emotional reaction may be a small trigger. It might be someone's accent or the type of words they use or the way they look at other people. One small switch will open up a canister of gas. One small trigger point might lead to an explosion in your inner emotions.

As you look at your future career it is worth asking what the emotional reactions are in you that can be destructive. What are the inner explosions that can happen and how can they be stopped or constrained? How can the energy that goes into an inner crossness be channelled in a more productive way so it leads to finding solutions rather than just recycling past prejudices?

Part of embracing simplicity is understanding your emotional reactions so you are not caught by those emotions in the same way as in the past. Sometimes a de-tox is about being released from captivity to ambition. You need to be liberated from the desire to attain what is now not possible. You need to let go of the emotions that drive you, and then reconstruct a view of the future that is free from the emotions of the past and the poison that can flow from resentment about unfulfilled ambition. Once we are liberated from past unrealistic ambitions, we might be able to see a future that is more attainable, more fulfilling and more joyful.

Marcia was captive to her emotions. She felt guilty about spending time at work when she would like to be with her family. She could feel put upon as a mum and taken for granted. At work she sometimes felt that the clients took advantage of her goodwill and gave her unrealistic deadlines because they had not been able to make their progress in good order. Sometimes the emotional reactions combined to create a mini inferno.

Marcia knew that the emotions could lead to poisonous attitudes that were destructive of her and her family. She recognized that she needed to take the emotions

---

out of situations more often. She kept telling herself, 'I must be level-headed and I must not let my emotions overwhelm me.' She recognized that when her emotions were in danger of overwhelming her, she needed to go outside for some fresh air: this could be a brisk fifteen-minute walk at lunchtime or one hour on a Saturday morning. Marcia knew what her safety valves were and how best she could turn them on.

Some points for reflection

- Recognize, in the organization where you work, what situations could be toxic and how best you can handle those situations.
- Recognize in yourself the mix of emotions that can lead to a mini explosion.
- Accept what are the most appropriate ways of handling your emotions so they are not destructive.
- Recognize the patterns of reactions in you that can lead to irrational behaviour.
- Be explicit with yourself about the steps you need to take to ensure you keep calm and objective and do not let poisonous emotions overcome you.

RENEW

PART 7

BRING A LIGHTNESS OF TOUCH

Mid-life and mid-career might mean that life can feel a bit heavy. You are carrying responsibilities that feel more like burdens than opportunities. There can be a relentlessness about the tasks facing you. It is like facing the headlights of a never-ending stream of traffic coming towards you. You can feel in the spotlight with little room for manoeuvre.

How do you bring a lightness of touch to situations that seem relentless and in danger of becoming overpowering? Perhaps it is about not taking yourself too seriously and accepting who you are. Handling relentlessness involves knowing what makes you smile and reinvigorates you. Bringing a lightness of touch can help you accept that some people are always going to be difficult to deal with, and can help you be prepared for situations where you might snap.

25

Don't take yourself too seriously and accept who you are

You may have been influenced by the management rhetoric about having a clear vision for how you want to contribute to an organization. The organization you are part of might have a clear mission statement or statement of purposes with which you have been identified. You have been brought up to believe the rhetoric of the organization or the profession of which you are part. Of course it is right to take those objectives seriously and be determined to make a difference in whatever sphere you are operating within.

But it can all become very serious. Your single-mindedness may well have been an asset in the past in getting things done. Being able to focus now on a key task is something that you get a lot of satisfaction from. But if you take life too seriously it can feel like disaster if your objectives are not delivered.

As a civil servant you are totally committed to delivering the objectives of the government of the day. But you have got to be able to accept that the next government may well have very different policies. You could find yourself unpicking the policies that you had been responsible for implementing a year or two earlier. To be able to live with a radical change of policy, you have to combine the serious intent to deliver what your political masters have requested, with then accepting with good humour that the mandate has changed. Keeping an equilibrium between serious intent and acceptance that the requirements might change is part of the inevitable balance that has to be sustained as a leader in a demanding role.

The best of leaders can laugh at themselves. They can recognize when they have made a point too strongly and reduce the intensity with which they take forward an argument. If you look too serious the people you want to influence may want to withdraw and not wish to be influenced by the points you make. When you can bring a lightness into serious points you are much more likely to be influential. Getting this balance right is much easier if you are prepared to blend lightness and seriousness.

You may have had a particular belief or attitude over many years, but perhaps that belief is now a shade outdated. You mouth the words but in your heart you have moved on. You are much more open to differences in religious, cultural and family perspectives. There are beliefs and attitudes to which you hold firmly, but you are much more open to accept the distinctiveness of other perspectives and embrace difference more readily than previous generations.

Accepting who you are is about recognizing your strengths and your foibles and going with the grain of your preferences. It is moving on from the 'try harder syndrome', which suggests that every problem is solved purely by trying harder. You are grown up enough to accept that you need to smile at your foibles and enjoy your strengths. There is a point in life, often in mid-life, when we become comfortable with who we are and are able to accept and enjoy the mix of characteristics that make up our personality. We know what situations we need to avoid because they bring out the worst in us, but we also know what situations will bring out the best in us.

Neil had felt a strong sense of vocation as chief executive of a small housing charity. He was earnest in his approach and felt strongly about the importance of

*advocating the cause of the charity. But he would speak
at considerable length. In committee meetings he tended
to be the dominant voice. Two of the charity trustees
collected feedback for Neil's performance review. Their
steers to him were that his commitment and enthusiasm were admired, but that his seriousness could put
people off. To maximize his effectiveness the feedback
was that he needed to become more focused in what he
said and bring much more lightness through examples
and through his tone of voice. In meetings he needed to
encourage others more and not be so serious in what he
said.*

*This was tough feedback for Neil to take. His initial
reaction was one of mild outrage. But the wise counsel of
his spouse was that he would wear himself out if he kept
up this heightened level of seriousness. Neil accepted that
he needed to calm down and take himself less seriously.
He accepted that he needed to bring more lightness into
his talks and into his wider contribution.*

Some points for reflection

- Be willing to laugh at yourself when your interventions
  do not quite land as you had wished.
- When people give you feedback, try to see the situation
  from their point of view.
- Observe how bringing humour into what you say makes
  you more influential.
- Reflect on what beliefs and attitudes you have held
  seriously may now need to be modified.
- Observe what makes you overserious and lose your
  sense of perspective.

26

Know what makes you smile and reinvigorates you and others

The ideas of a younger leader in the organization may inspire you or depress you. You may think they bring a freshness that is to be encouraged. Or your first reaction might be that we tried that before and it is unlikely to work on this occasion.

Sometimes there might even be a touch of resentment about why they have thought of this and not me. Why is this younger leader going to be more successful than I have been? When a younger leader has a good idea, our first reaction might be to try to trump that idea and come up with an even better one. When we feel a touch of resentment or competitiveness perhaps the most helpful initial response is to smile at our reaction and let that smile dampen any emotional reactions that might otherwise dominate.

As a younger leader begins to blossom there is a choice in the attitude you take. It can either be one of encouragement and support or one of feeling slightly threatened and keeping your distance. Enabling others to bring the best out of themselves can be a contribution that makes you smile and enables the whole organization to thrive.

The organization of which you are part may be going through tough times. The demands of customers and clients may seem overwhelming. Or the bureaucracy imposed by government may seem unwieldy and senseless, but you know that you cannot change the situation. You might be able to influence the way external expectations are interpreted within the organization.

You may be able to push back on the expectations of senior management and agree a much clearer set of priorities, but the external factors may be such that you have to live with the deadlines or form-filling that is externally imposed. All you can do is understand the context, take it step by step and then try to smile at the situation you are in.

Whatever the demands of the day and however gloomy the future looks, it helps if at the end of the day you are able to ask yourself the question, 'What made me smile today?' There will always have been something that caught your imagination, an event that had the touch of the ridiculous about it, a comment from a colleague that brought a touch of a smile to your face.

When you see that a meeting is flat or people are getting bored, a contribution that can have a profound effect might be a gentle comment that enables others to smile or puts what is happening in the room into a wider perspective. Often what reinvigorates people is not the call to 'try harder' but words of praise about what has been achieved or comments of encouragement about what is attainable going forward.

You may think that you are not the leader who is best equipped to set out a clear vision. Your energy may be less than others'. But if from your experience and understanding of the people around you, you can help them see a wider perspective and come to believe that progress is attainable, you are bringing a precious gift of invigorating others. Bringing lightness does not only benefit you. It can re-energize those around you, enabling a team to laugh at itself and thereby feel more connected for the future. It is a precious contribution. The quiet influence of bringing a lightness of touch is a precious gift that the mature, experienced leader can bring in a self-effacing and effective way.

Neil was brought up to believe that advocacy is a serious business and that he was being disrespectful to the cause if he smiled too much. He was bringing a serious message

117

that needed to be listened to seriously. When he was with his family he smiled a lot. But in public he could take on a preaching voice. Neil's spouse kept suggesting to him that he use more of the storytelling approach that worked so successfully with his family. Reluctantly he incorporated more stories and allowed his humour to show through more. He began to tell gentle jokes against himself when he was speaking in front of people.

Neil began to get feedback that was much warmer. People remembered his stories and began to tell them back to him. Part of him was sceptical about whether he was using the right approach, but he observed that his leadership team meetings were becoming more lively. There was more energy in the room and more creativity about the ideas they were discussing for the future. In the meetings he was increasingly willing to laugh at himself. Others commented that they were becoming more invigorated, and the meetings were more productive combined with a stronger sense of common purpose.

Some points for reflection

- What prompts you to smile at yourself?
- What type of contribution from you can reinvigorate groups of which you are part?
- How can you use humour to diffuse tense situations?
- What frequency might work for you in reviewing what has made you smile over the past week or day?
- How might you use humour to help reinvigorate different meetings of which you are part?

27

Accept that some people are difficult to deal with

As we grow more experienced we think that we will become more adept at dealing with difficult people. We have learnt to control our emotional reactions to people who annoy us. We have learnt that people have different preferences and behave in different ways related to their experiences and their personalities.

We have learnt not to provoke people who are easily offended. We recognize the signals in people when they are about to lose their cool and say things that are likely to be destructive and harmful. We have decided to ignore some people because they come over to us as self-opinionated and unwilling to listen.

Sometimes it is a necessary challenge to seek to win over someone who is being difficult. We cannot ignore the difficult parent, patient, customer, client or union representative. Sustaining leadership over a long period requires winning round difficult people. It can be helpful to see this as a planned exercise where you are deliberately deploying different tactics and seeing which works. Spending time with difficult people where we listen to their perspective is often worth the investment. Flattery often wins people round as you acknowledge the positive contribution they have made. Asking a difficult person for advice can mean that they open up and give a perspective that is wider than you might have anticipated.

Working together with people who appear to you to be difficult is often an inevitability. Where you are part of a team with those you find difficult you have to find ways of sustaining yourself without difficult relationships draining your energy. This can mean putting up emotional barriers so the barbs or comments of another person do not wind you up or wound you. It might mean trying to find a common purpose whereby you and the individual you find difficult can work together in a way that draws on your respective strengths to deliver a particular purpose.

Sometimes when a relationship is very difficult between you and a colleague it is right to surface the issue and seek mediation so that a way forward can be found for both the organization, you and the other individual. Letting undercurrents fester usually leads to a bigger problem and a more explosive outcome.

If someone who works for you is very difficult, your priority is likely to be setting clear objectives and monitoring both performance and attitudes. If it is a peer who is difficult, progress can come through agreeing areas where there can be co-operative working together. If your boss is a difficult person to deal with, developing a joint approach with your colleagues can be a productive way forward.

Neil recognized that in any voluntary organization there will be some people who will be resistant to change and others who will feel aggrieved if they do not get their own way. He recognized that some of the older volunteers would be resistant to change and carefully talked through his reasons for making changes with these individuals. He devoted time to projects that these people were particularly interested in: he recognized that he needed to keep their support because of their important contribution to the overall charity and to its financial security. Most of this group Neil took with him. A couple remained strongly opposed: Neil recognized that that was as good a conclusion as he was going to get.

One of the trustees had very fixed views. Neil welcomed this person's energy but could foresee conflict if he could not reach agreement about how this energy was best directed. This person knew some members of the community well and responded positively to the suggestion that he work closely with some specific groups. What might have been a difficult relationship became one that worked perfectly adequately, with this individual focusing on a discrete and important element of the charity's work. Experience had taught Neil that he would always have to work with people who appeared difficult to him. He recognized that there would be people who found him difficult too. This was a fact of life that had to be accepted.

Some points for reflection

- Accept that there will always be some people you will find difficult.
- Plan carefully in dealing with difficult people in terms of how you might turn them around.
- Build common cause with others in handling difficult people effectively.
- Recognize what emotional armour you need to put on to protect yourself from people who can be poisonous.
- Be willing to challenge difficult people sometimes, and sometimes deliberately walk away.

28

Be prepared for when you might snap

My elder son does ironman triathlons that involve swimming, cycling long distances and then running a marathon. He talks of the importance of a clear focus on different milestones and being sustained through regular nourishment. The successful triathlete is both pushing themselves and knowing how they live within their own physical, mental and emotional resources. They develop a rhythm that they are able to live within and know when they need to take in liquid and food to keep that rhythm going.

The triathlete is sustaining their momentum through the mental picture of the end goal, the sense of shared endeavour through fellow competitors alongside them, emotional uplifting through the cheers of supporters and regular physical sustenance from water, fruit and energy bars.

Being sustained as a leader over a long period requires the same inputs of clarity of goal, emotional support and physical sustenance. The triathlete is surprised how far their forward motion takes them when they are in a rhythm. As a leader you can be sustained far longer than you might anticipate through careful planning and knowing how you are best sustained intellectually, emotionally and physically.

The good triathlete knows when they have to slow down to ease the pain or to take in sustenance. They recognize the points where they might snap and know not to go up to that point. Where a hill has to be tackled it is better to do it more slowly than rush up the incline to be completely exhausted at its summit. Keeping sustained as a leader over the long haul is about pacing how you use your energy. It is rarely rushing at things.

Success comes through carefully planned strategies and bringing an adaptability when obstacles are bigger than you had originally expected. There are moments when it is right to say, 'I am not going to take the direct pathway to the top of that hill; I am going to take a more secure route that is more likely to guarantee my arrival at the destination.'

The good triathlete keeps training and anticipates the situations they will need to overcome so that they are not caught unawares. The leader who is sustained through tough times is the leader who has planned carefully and is balancing their capabilities alongside the tasks that need to be done.

Neil was conscious that as chief executive he had been encouraging a lot of initiatives by different groups. All these initiatives needed some of his time. A couple of the projects were being led in a slightly half-hearted way. Neil wanted to be directive and be more insistent about progress, but he recognized that he was working with volunteers and could make suggestions but could not be insistent. He recognized that he was in danger of becoming impatient with those leading these two projects but also recognized that it would be counter-productive if he sent a critical e-mail.

Neil accepted that he needed to talk to the two project leaders to understand their concern and to find a way ahead that they were able to handle and to which they were willing to be fully committed. He talked openly with each individual about their hopes for the project

---

and the time they could realistically commit. The out-
come was that one project leader withdrew while the
other became more committed and took the project on
in a more purposeful way to its next phase.

Some points for reflection

- Recognize that you have to settle into a rhythm that will last over an extended period.
- Recognize what sustains you intellectually, emotionally and physically over the long haul.
- Accept that there are moments when it is crucial to turn down the pace for the benefit of long-term sustainability.
- Keep focused on the goals you want to attain while being ready to adapt the route and the pacing to get there.
- When it all gets too much, rest for a while and then dust yourself off, being clear what you have learnt and what is going to sustain you going forward.

PART 8

BUILD FOR THE FUTURE

It is always worth building for the future, whatever stage in your career or your life journey you are currently at. You may feel unenthusiastic about what the future might hold. You might feel locked into your current situation and unable to see different opportunities opening up. Perhaps the future is about holding on to what you have got and making the most of limited physical or financial resources.

In this part I encourage you to look at what might be possible in the future. The chapters address exploring new avenues, building your supporters, recognizing your safety net and being willing to trust your instincts. Going forward there are always choices to be made about your attitudes and about how you deploy the time, however limited, that is available to you.

29

Explore new avenues

Three miles away from where we live is Winkworth Arboretum, which in the spring shows off its magnificent magnolias, azaleas and bluebell woods. In the autumn the trees are a blaze of red and orange leaves. A network of footpaths cuts across woodland areas and takes you up and down the slopes. When the children were little we had a rendezvous point overlooking the lake, with the children going on their own 'secret' paths to get to this destination. As the children got older they wanted to explore new paths through the arboretum. When we visit the arboretum now the paths are the same ones we walked on thirty years ago but the colours and vegetation are always different. On every visit there is something new to look at that captures our imagination.

When we feel staid and a bit stuck there are probably still new avenues we can explore. Through the internet our access to information about any subject is almost unlimited. There are networks we can join that focus on a wide range of different interests. We can begin to take an interest in a different sport, we can delve more deeply into interesting theology, philosophy, literature or art. Developing an interest in a particular artist or composer can inspire us in our personal lives and also in our work.

I first did a long-distance walk taking over a week some ten years ago and have now done sixteen and completed some of them two or three times. Doing the long walks has introduced me to new places, helped to keep me fit physically and given me many metaphors that I am able to use in coaching individuals, teams and groups.

Might there be a new interest that would catch your imagination and give you ideas across the whole of your life? There is always time to commit half an hour to explore a particular avenue that keeps you alert to what is happening in the fast-changing world and brings freshness in the way you look at life and to your attitudes to other people.

A starting point is to reflect on the skills and interests you bring that are potentially transferable. If you enjoy contributing to meetings, can you contribute to a wider range of meetings on different subjects? If you are good at writing, can you transfer those gifts into different spheres, possibly becoming secretary of a local society or governing body? As you explore new avenues and potentially take on some commitments outside work, it helps keep you and your CV fresh.

The potential employer who is looking at taking on someone in mid-life is going to want to be assured that they bring a liveliness of current interests and a willingness to take on responsibilities, alongside both experience and a freshness of approach. If you are demonstrating in the different aspects of your life that you are able to transfer experiences and competences into different activities then you are more likely to be seen as adaptable and able to take on new commitments.

Keeping fresh is both about exploring new avenues and seeing the light differently as you walk down a path you tread every week. The more you can see changes and freshness on a journey you travel regularly, the more alert you are to new ways of seeing the world and opportunities that might open up that will rekindle your energy and use your gifts to best effect.

Barbara had led a general practitioner practice for a few years. She enjoyed seeing patients and was broadly content with the administrative responsibilities of leading the practice. Her working life was reasonably predictable. There were always problems in the surgery that needed to be solved but they were mostly manageable without being too stressful. Barbara knew she had to explore new avenues to keep herself fresh. She decided to take a bigger interest in preventative measures and got engaged in some local public-health initiatives.

Her children were now at university and so she had more time for her personal interests. Barbara began to play golf once a week. She had always been interested in the ethics of medicine and decided to look at some of the theological and philosophical issues that impinged on medical ethics. She made herself available to spend a couple of mornings each spring at the local sixth-form college to talk to youngsters who wanted to think through whether medicine was the right career for them. Doing this combination of different, new activities helped to keep Barbara fresh in her day job as head of the GP practice.

Some points for reflection

- What new avenues in terms of work interests might be available to you?
- How much time can you commit to following up new personal interests and what might you take forward?
- How might you view the journeys you do on a regular basis in a different way so you are more alert to what is going on around you?
- How might you use your gifts and competences in different spheres on a voluntary basis to help keep you fresh and to demonstrate the transferability of your skills?

30

Build your supporters

The frequent advice in mid-life is to keep building your networks because you never know when these networks might be useful to you. The growth in social networks provides a mechanism to exchange information with a wide range of different people. The risk is that we are deluged with information; also these networks are superficial and ultimately unrewarding.

I have deliberately entitled this chapter 'Build your supporters' rather than 'Build your networks'. Someone who supports you is someone with whom there is an intellectual and emotional connection. A supporter is somebody who thinks well of you and wants the best for you. A supporter will be encouraging and will be willing to help you. Their commitment to you is much more than the passing interest prompted by the push of one button on a social network site.

We build supporters by giving rather than demanding to receive. When we give someone our sole, undivided attention and show an interest in their priorities, we are building a connectivity that is a source of encouragement to both parties. The more you show yourself committed to someone's wellbeing and success, the more they are willing to think well of you. If the only reason to show interest in people is to build their support for you, the shallowness of your intent is likely to show through. Support for you from others only flows when you have demonstrated genuine and unconditional encouragement and support for them.

Building your supporters might be about finding a common cause. It may include working jointly with people from different backgrounds and in different age groups so that you demonstrate your ability to work effectively in diverse teams and you build supporters from different spheres who recognize and will speak well of your competences and experiences.

It is worth asking who your supporters are and what they will say about you. It can be worth your asking them what the generic skills are that you bring that they see as transferable to other organizations. Sound advice from supporters can stop you going in the wrong direction and encourage you to explore avenues you had not previously considered.

If you keep asking the question, 'Who can I learn from?', that intent will bring you into more intimate contact with people you admire. The more you are willing to learn from people, the more they are likely to become your supporters.

The good supporter is not someone who tells you what you want to hear. The good supporter will tell you the truth about what is realistic and to where you might most effectively address your energies. Part of maintaining supporters is saying thank you and recognizing their contribution on a regular basis. This is not about excessive flattery or being ingratiating. It is about the genuine acknowledgement of the contribution of those who are committed to your success.

Another angle is being able to build up a relationship quickly with someone so that you have their support even though you have had very little contact with them. The art of giving someone your sole, undivided attention and finding points of shared interest is likely to lead to emotional warmth that provides the first step to building mutual support. The ability to build a connection quickly so that people who meet you for the first time leave that conversation thinking well of you is a gift well worth cultivating.

Barbara was well known as the head of a GP practice but did not have a profile in the public-health world. Some people were wary of her because they feared she would want to be dominant in the discussions about future, preventative health measures. Barbara deliberately visited those with a public-health interest, asking them questions and building a personal rapport. She did not rush to express her own views.

Barbara's approach was to build on what others told her and play back the evidence she was hearing. She rapidly built the support of a wide group of people involved in public health. When a decision was needed about who was going to the vice chair of the public health planning committee, Barbara was the obvious choice because she had built a good level of rapport with a cross section of specialists with different interests.

Some points for reflection

- Who might you support and encourage in the work they are doing?
- With whom can you build a stronger sense of shared interest?
- Whose support would you particularly welcome and how can you support them?
- How can you best develop the ability to build rapport quickly with people you are meeting for the first time?
- Who might you explicitly thank for their support and encouragement of you?

31

Recognize your safety net

The trapeze artist is willing to try amazing moves because they have the safety net below them. The intrepid rock-climber is bolder than they might otherwise have been because they are harnessed and attached firmly to the top of the cliff. The soldier jumps from the aeroplane enjoying the free fall because he knows that as soon as he presses the button the parachute will open up. The crew member hangs over the edge of the boat in the knowledge that they are attached by a safety harness.

As you try new approaches or go out of your comfort zone to explore different options, what is your safety net? Sometimes it might be the existing job or role. You may not be entirely satisfied with where you are currently working, but you recognize the value of applying for a job from within a job. You do not want to risk the uncertainty of having no role as you apply for different roles. Because of family responsibilities you may be very clear that until you have another role you are not prepared to resign from your current position.

On other occasions no such safety net exists. Your job has come to an end and there is no immediate safety net. In this situation your safety net may be some hard-earned savings and some activities in the voluntary sector that do not pay the bills but keep you sane and reasonably positive about life.

At times of uncertainty about work your safety nets might be your family, your friends and your faith. Members of your family will love you anyway and will want to support you in the best way they can. The best of your friends will be available to talk through with you what you are experiencing. They will be sources of encouragement and will take you into other areas of interest so you are not completely preoccupied by your own misfortune. Your faith, if you have one, will enable you to put into a wider context your own individual experience and should help reduce the feeling of being overwhelmed by adversity.

In advance of needing a safety net it can be worth reflecting on what safety nets you are building. Are you investing enough in your pension? Are you investing in your own continuous professional development so you are marketable if your current role comes to an end? Are you involved in leadership roles outside the narrow work environment so that your CV demonstrates your initiative and the width of leadership capabilities that you bring?

If you are in a line of work that has a professional association, is it worth investing more time in that association so that you are building an understanding of future trends and developing supporters in other organizations? This does not give you a guarantee of future employment, but it provides a good basis of contacts and credibility from which to start.

The most important safety net is provided by those people who love you most deeply. Keeping investing in these people through your own interest, love and care is by far the most important way of building the type of safety net that will keep you going if your work world feels as if it is falling apart.

Barbara knew that one of the other doctors in the practice was keen to succeed her as head of the practice. Barbara enjoyed both the responsibility and the status of leading the practice and was reluctant to conceive of moving on from this role. She felt a sense of mild humiliation when a couple of her colleagues suggested she should stand down. Her initial reaction was to protest and assert herself even more. But she knew she was cherished by her family and increasingly respected in the public-health community.

Barbara decided to stand down before she was pushed by her colleagues. She overcame her hurt pride reasonably quickly, partly because of the teasing of her husband and a couple of good friends. The love she shared with her husband, the good companionship of her friends and the pleasure of developing her interest in public health were the safety nets that allowed her to move on and shift the focus of her leadership away from the GP practice and into wider public-health issues across the community.

Some points for reflection

- What are the safety nets that are most important to you?
- How do you keep your safety nets strong and effective?
- How do you want to invest in the safety nets that are going to be most important to you over future years?
- Can you acknowledge even more strongly those people who currently act as safety nets for you?
- In what ways can you create a safety net for other people who are important to you?

32

Trust your instincts

At times of uncertainty about the future we may be deluged with advice. The comments will always be well intended. There may be one suggestion after another about what we might do next and how our skills and experience can be used in different ways.

Professional advisers such as head hunters, others in a similar area of work or career counsellors may put before us a wealth of possibilities. Most of the ideas may seem unrealistic. We feel caught in a maze and unable to make meaningful progress.

Perhaps we need space to let the different possibilities and ideas either take shape or disappear. Perhaps we have to let our unconscious brain do its own thinking to see which ideas we forget and which tend to recur. If we tell ourselves that we want to explore two or three possibilities, our unconscious brain may well distil the information it has received into two or three possibilities. One approach is to say to yourself before going to sleep that in the morning you will decide on two or three possibilities you are going to take further forward. Perhaps surprisingly, although not inevitably, your brain will have followed the instruction you gave it and distilled possibilities down to two or three.

A couple of years ago I had dinner with someone in their late twenties whose business idea was not working out as they had hoped. This person was very uncertain about what sort of career she should try to embark upon. I invited her to score different possible options out of ten. The request was to give an intuitive and immediate score. Most options she scored as two

136

or three out of ten. When I mentioned teaching she immediately said eight. She was taken aback by her intuitive response. She talked through the idea of teaching in more detail, applied successfully to go on a PGCE course and then began teaching primary-school children a year later. She had found her new vocation. What set off this new direction was the drawing out of an intuitive scoring and then testing that option.

We are using our intuitive responses all the time. As you think about the future, being honest about your preferences and how you might use them is a good starting point. Asking yourself what intuitively you think is the right next thing to explore is not an indulgent question. It is based on a recognition that the wealth of experiences that you have informs your intuitive sense. What is important is the ability to talk through your intuitive responsibilities with trusted others who can help you to understand the rationale between those intuitive responses and the extent to which emotional considerations might be distorting those first reactions.

When Barbara saw a job advertised in public health she surprised herself by her fascination of what the job would be like. She enjoyed being a GP and had a secure income. Moving out of general practice into public-health work would be a major change. She would not be as equipped as other candidates for the post, but her intuitive sense was that she had a lot to offer and could build a very strong public-health agenda in her area.

Barbara tested her intuitive reaction with some other doctors and with her family. Financially she would be slightly worse off, but that seemed a small consideration when compared with the job interest. Perhaps it was a waste in some ways to leave the general practice but her intuitive sense was telling her that moving full time into public health would bring a new freshness and give her another phase of working life where she could make a significant contribution to the wider community. Barbara was unhesitating in going for this role and was delighted when she was appointed.

Some points for reflection

- How much do you trust your instincts when it comes to your future work?
- With whom can you test out the robustness of your instincts?
- How best do you move into reflective space where you can explore your intuitive feelings about future options?
- How best can you ask your brain questions and then give it time to process those questions and give you some considered answers?
- What is the pattern for you that works best in terms of identifying and then testing out your intuitive preferences?

PART 9

KEEP SUSTAINED

This part sets out a framework that can be used to help keep you sustained over the long haul. It is intended as a framework that you can come back to on a regular basis. The intention is to create a virtuous circle in which you *reflect*, *reframe*, *rebalance* and *renew*.

The purpose of this part is to set out some questions and actions that might enable you to stand back and observe what is happening to you, and then move forward in a way that is measured, constructive and hopeful about the future.

Keeping sustained requires finding the approaches that are going to work for you. It is never about accepting someone else's solution wholesale. Do take account of your preferences and your past experiences to develop a methodology that works for you so that you keep sustained intellectually, emotionally, physically and spiritually over the next phase of your work and life.

33

Reflect

A key starting point is taking time to reflect. Elements of reflection might include:

- What is the new reality I need to address?
- What elements of my past experience do I need to reassess to see how relevant they are to the future?
- Do I need to recalculate the progress I have made towards the explicit or implicit objectives I had set myself?
- Might I usefully remember some of the previous paths I have been on to see whether I see the world in a different light with the benefit of life's experience?

As you reflect on your journey so far you might:

- Recall some of the good memories that cheer and embolden you.
- Remember those who were sources of encouragement and taught you what you understand about life and its meaning.
- Recognize how your family and cultural background have shaped you and given you a view of the world that colours everything you see and do.
- Be ready to reshape your expectations that date from childhood and youth that ought now to be left behind.

When Alan Smith and I wrote *The Reflective Leader* we talked about the importance of being able to 'stand and stare', recognizing 'what lights your fire' and having 'good companions on the way'. As you reflect on your leadership journey so far and your next steps, I encourage you to:

- Be willing to stand still and to look back on the progress you have made.
- Look around you to stand and stare and observe the journeys of others and what you learn from them.
- Think about what has 'lit your fire' in years past and the extent to which that fire is still there or can be rekindled going forward.
- Recognize who have been the companions on the way who have been most influential upon you, and the extent to which there is a continuing companionship that you can draw from that will help sustain you over the next few years.

It is worth thinking about what is the right context to encourage reflection. Perhaps it is to visit a favourite place, go on a long walk, go on a retreat or have focused conversations with a good companion or coach. Good-quality reflection is not indulgence, rather it is bringing an openness to review the past and see how it speaks into the future so that you can thoughtfully and openly address the questions:

- What mountains do I want to climb?
- What do I want to leave behind?
- Where does work fit into the rest of life?
- What difference do I want to make in different spheres in my life?

34

Reframe

When a picture is reframed the colours in it can have a new life because of the blending tones in the mount or the frame. When you look at a view from a different angle you are reframing what you are seeing. When you alter the aperture on a camera the scene that appeared dull can come out as much brighter and more enticing.

Having reflected on the significance of the past it is helpful to reframe it as you look to the future. Elements of this might be to:

- Re-address what previous beliefs and attitudes might be holding you back.
- Consciously decide which aspects of your inherited beliefs and experiences you intend to retain and which you intend to leave behind.
- Be thoughtful about who are the types of people and situations that will refresh your sense of purpose and enthusiasm about life and give you new angles and perspectives.
- Decide how best you want to rekindle a zest for living and a desire to experiment and overcome obstacles so you are ready for opportunities ahead.

Looking to the future might also mean you need to:

- Reformulate your expectations of yourself.
- Re-brand any of your distinctive characteristics that you previously thought held you back.

- Reconstruct your self-image so negative feelings about your background and your previous contribution are replaced by a more positive view about what you have learnt and how you propose to use that learning going forward.
- Consciously decide what responsibilities you are going to move on from to give you the capacity to take forward new interests or responsibilities that are now more important to you.

Practical ways of looking to the future might include asking questions like:

- Who are the people who are going to be most important to me over the next ten years and how do I want to contribute to their wellbeing?
- What types of activities are going to give me the greatest levels of fulfilment going forward?
- What type of success is important to me over the next ten years and why?
- What are the hopes and fears for me in the minds and hearts of those who are closest to me?
- Who do I know who has reframed their past and is looking to the future in a way I admire? What can I learn from them?
- In what ways is current adversity enabling me to reframe what is important to me in a way that is constructive and helpful for the future?
- How am I going to handle potential derailers going forward when events go wrong and stress builds up?
- How might I reframe my beliefs about the future so I can anticipate making a positive contribution to others' wellbeing in a way that is more enabling and less competitive than in the past?

The exercise of reframing might benefit from looking at the future through the eyes of different family members and having constructive dialogue with trusted friends about the future and your potential place in that future. Reframing might involve turning upside down some of your current beliefs and attitudes. But it might also involve becoming clearer about what are the beliefs, relationships and fixed points that are most important to you going forward.

35

Rebalance

After reflecting on the journey so far and reframing what the future might look like, there can be the opportunity to rebalance priorities and the use of time and energy. Elements of this might include a decision to:

- Reconnect with people, interests and organizations that are going to be important to you going forward.
- Redirect your priorities into areas where you want to make a difference and have the right capabilities to make an effective contribution.
- Reposition the way you contribute in your work so that you have the type of impact you want.
- Retrain your brain through adding new skills or practising arts that you want to develop further.

Rebalancing may involve some quite demanding changes in the way you do things and organize your time and energy. It might involve decisions to:

- Reshape your working day so you make the best use of your time when you are fresh to work on longer-term priorities.
- Reinvigorate your thinking through what you read and through dialogue with people who stimulate your imagination and interest.

- Recreate the type of contexts where your thinking is at its freshest and most adventurous.
- Revise those fixed assumptions that limit what you believe is possible going forward.

Rebalancing is a never-ending process. Changes in family circumstances and physical and emotional wellbeing will necessitate adjustments to the personal equilibrium that work for you. What matters is being deliberate in recognizing what needs to change and doing it in a timely way. Rebalancing will often mean making a firm decision to stop doing some tasks and ending certain responsibilities. But it will always mean thinking about what is changing and what are the new interests, attitudes or perspectives it is right to embrace.

Rebalancing may not be about moving from one fixed position to another. It might incorporate adaptability to an evolving situation and a recognition that sustaining your leadership will involve flexing the way you use your talents, time and energy depending on the varying requirements from home, family and work.

As you reflect on rebalancing the way you look at the world, practical questions might include:

- What are your current physical and emotional trigger points and limitations?
- How much flexibility is important to you?
- What are the fixed points and milestones going forward that are not for rebalancing?
- What are the views of significant others in your life on what and how you might rebalance?
- How do you ensure you always stay professional and focused when you go through a bad patch or others overtake you?
- How can you embrace simplicity, so that you de-clutter, de-complicate, de-mystify, and de-tox?

36

Renew

At the heart of sustaining leadership is the belief that there is always the opportunity to renew and reshape the future. The family that is strong nurtures its young people so that the family is continually renewed through succeeding generations. The organization that survives and thrives will have values that bind it together but it will be continually renewing its aspirations and the way it develops the best in people.

What might be the elements of renewal in the way leadership can be sustained over a long period even when buffeted by a range of external pressures? Elements involved in renewal might include the need to:

- Rebuild practical aspects of the way you live so there is space and time to bring sustained leadership.
- Revitalize your hopes for the future so that they are practical aspirations and not unattainable dreams.
- Re-energize, physically, emotionally, intellectually and spiritually so that you are always reflecting on new insights.
- Resuscitate your heartbeat where you have lost the passion for aspects of life that are important to you.

As you renew your hopes and aspirations for the future you might want to decide to:

- Recharge your enthusiasm in particular areas.

- Re-examine what is holding you back and decide what you need to jettison.
- Be open to yourself and those closest to you about what your preferences are for the future.
- Restate the anchor points about your beliefs and attitudes that are non-negotiable for the future.

Regular renewal of our thinking, our beliefs, our attitudes and the relationships that are most important to us is essential to living vibrant, sustained lives. As leaders we have a responsibility to ourselves and to others to allow ourselves to be open to renewal, alert to changes around us and willing to bring a freshness of thinking. But renewal always involves being abundantly clear about what is important.

Practical ways of thinking constructively about how you keep renewed as a leader might be stimulated by the following questions:

- What will help bring a lightness of touch and a smile to your face so you do not take yourself or others too seriously?
- Who stimulates your thinking and enables you to think in fresh ways about the future?
- What written texts from literature, poetry or Scripture uplift you and help take you into new ways of thinking?
- What types of reflection, reframing and rebalancing will enable you to renew the sense of purpose and hopefulness within you?

My encouragement to you is to take the initiative yourself to sustain your own leadership and renew it. Cast aside negative attitudes from the past and a weariness about the present as you reflect on the gifts you have been given. Reframe the realities and opportunities around you. Rebalance your expectations and priorities. Renew the sense of purpose and hopefulness within you.

Books by Peter Shaw

Mirroring Jesus as Leader, Cambridge: Grove, 2004.

Conversation Matters: How to Engage Effectively with One Another, London: Continuum, 2005.

The Four Vs of Leadership: Vision, Values, Value-added, and Vitality, Chichester: Capstone, 2006.

Finding Your Future: The Second Time around, London: Darton, Longman & Todd, 2006.

Business Coaching: Achieving Practical Results through Effective Engagement, Chichester: Capstone, 2007 (co-authored with Robin Linnecar).

Making Difficult Decisions: How to be Decisive and Get the Business Done, Chichester: Capstone, 2008.

Deciding Well: A Christian Perspective on Making Decisions as a Leader, Vancouver: Regent College Publishing, 2009.

Raise Your Game: How to Succeed at Work, Chichester: Capstone, 2009.

Effective Christian Leaders in the Global Workplace, Colorado Springs: Authentic/Paternoster, 2010.

Defining Moments: Navigating through Business and Organizational Life, Basingstoke: Palgrave/Macmillan, 2010.

The Reflective Leader: Standing Still to Move Forward, Norwich: Canterbury Press, 2011 (co-authored with Alan Smith).

Thriving in Your Work: How to be Motivated and Do Well in Challenging Times, London: Marshall Cavendish, 2011.

Getting the Balance Right: Leading and Managing Well, London: Marshall Cavendish, 2013.

Leading in Demanding Times, Grove, 2013 (co-authored with Graham Shaw).

The Emerging Leader: Stepping Up in Leadership, Norwich: Canterbury Press, 2013 (co-authored with Colin Shaw).

100 Great Personal Impact Ideas, London: Marshall Cavendish, 2013.

100 Great Coaching Ideas, London: Marshall Cavendish 2014.

Celebrating Your Senses, Delhi: ISPCK, 2014.

Sustaining Leadership, Norwich: Canterbury Press, 2014.

Forthcoming books
100 Great Team Effectiveness Ideas, London: Marshall Cavendish, 2015.

Effective Leadership Teams: A Christian Perspective, London: Darton, Longman & Todd, 2015 (co-authored with Judy Hurst).